LAUGH AND LEARN
BIBLE FOR KIDS

Written by **Phil Vischer**

Illustrated by **Michael K. Foster**

Presented to _____

By _____

On _____

TABLE of CONTENTS

FaithWords
Hachette Book Group, Inc.
1290 Avenue of the Americas, New York, NY 10104

hachettebookgroup.com | faithwords.com | laughandlearnbible.com

Written by Phil Vischer
Illustrated by Michael K. Foster

Editorial Director: Jessica Wolstenholm
Creative Director: Anne Fogerty
Art Director: John Trent
Lead Colorist: Joe Spadaford
Colorists: James Peñafiel, Amanda Wood
Designer: Mimi Roberts

Bible facts, historical context, and theology reviewed by Docent Research Group.

Library of Congress Cataloging-in-Publication Data has been applied for.

10 9 8 7 6 5 4 3 2
ISBN: 978-1-5460-1195-8 (Hardcover), 978-1-5460-1194-1 (eBook)
Printed in China
APS

WELCOME

I've been telling stories from the Bible to kids for more than twenty-five years now, first through VeggieTales® and more recently through projects like the Buck Denver Asks®. . . What's in the Bible? video series. Videos are a great way to introduce Bible stories to kids. *But what's the next step?* Jumping from a lighthearted video straight into Mom and Dad's old King James Version of the Bible is a **HUGE** leap for a child!

That's where this new storybook Bible comes in. My goal with the writing of these stories was to make the entire flow of Scripture accessible to kids in a form that encourages **FUN**, intergenerational reading—quality time with parents, grandparents, and caregivers.

So cozy up in a comfy chair with a child that you love, and start a journey together through God's **WORD**! In these pages you'll find the truth of the gospel, shaped into bite-sized nuggets that will hold your child's attention. Read your favorite stories one at a time or follow God's Story chronologically from Creation to Revelation to help your child understand God's love and rescue plan. We've added lots of extra content to help you connect the dots and make faith **REAL** for the next generation.

I hope you enjoy!

Phil Vischer

How to Use the Laugh and Learn Bible

Choose a Bible story to read together. After you laugh and learn through the story, check out these other ways to dig deeper into God's Word.

USE THE FAMILY CONNECTION AT THE END OF THE STORY.

- Read TRICKY BITS for answers to tough questions.
- Discuss FUN FACTS for details and context.
- Memorize the EVERYDAY TRUTH!
- TALK about the story using the prompts provided.
- PRAY together and ask God to help His truth take root in your heart.

USE THE BONUS CONTENT TO LEARN MORE.

- Read each Bible section introduction for context clues.
- Join Israel on their journey to the Promised Land (page 96).
- Learn about amazing women of the Bible (page 178).
- Discover Bible facts and memorize its books (page 224).
- Trace God's family tree from Abraham to Jesus (page 228).
- Follow Paul's missionary journeys (page 316).

READ THE BIBLE FROM CREATION TO REVELATION.

The *Laugh and Learn Bible* includes fifty-two stories for a reason. Read one five-minute story each week and you'll journey through the Bible in one year! The gospel is threaded intentionally through these stories. When read chronologically, the *Laugh and Learn Bible* clearly teaches God's rescue plan and the good news of Jesus' love!

THE PENTATEUCH

PENTATEUCH is a big, fancy word, but all it really means is "five books." The first five books of the Bible are called the Pentateuch. The Pentateuch tells the story of how God's relationship with people started out **GOOD** but was broken by **SIN**. The rest of the Bible is God's rescue plan to fix that relationship.

In these first five books, we see God make special friendships with a few people in order to **RESTORE** His friendship with all people. But these special friendships weren't enough.

The stories of the Pentateuch are only the beginning: the **FOUNDATION**. The rest of the Bible will build on everything we learn about God in these five books.

If you stopped reading the Bible here, you might think there was no hope for human beings. But every one of these foundational stories points us ahead to the rest of God's great **STORY**. Just like any story, without a foundation, the rest of it doesn't make much sense.

As we read the Pentateuch, we can see over and over again just how much God **LOVES** us. So much that He sent His Son Jesus to die for us (John 3:16).

But that comes later in the story. Let's start at the very beginning.

THE PENTATEUCH

Genesis Exodus Leviticus Numbers Deuteronomy

The Pentateuch points to Jesus as the **ONLY WAY** to fix our broken relationship with God. In the Pentateuch:

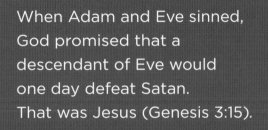

When Adam and Eve sinned, God promised that a descendant of Eve would one day defeat Satan. That was Jesus (Genesis 3:15).

When God saved the Israelites from slavery in Egypt, He told them to cover their doorways with the blood of a Lamb to represent a later sacrifice. That was Jesus (Exodus 12:5; John 1:29).

When God gave Moses the Law, He promised that one day, a prophet like no other would come who would fulfill the Law. That was Jesus (Deuteronomy 18:15–19).

CREATION

GOD

In the beginning, there was God.

Just God. Nothing else.

No trees, no hummingbirds, no ants, no stars, no galaxies, no mountains, no whales, no bats, no kids, no grown-ups, no grandmas or grandpas, no caterpillars, no lakes, no oceans, no horses, no elephants, and no frogs. Not even little tiny ones.

Just God.

You might think He was lonely in all that nothingness. But God wasn't lonely, because God wasn't alone.

You see, God is like us in some ways. He thinks. He feels. He acts. But in other ways He is very, very different.

God is everywhere. He knows everything. He is never wrong. **EVER**. And one other way God is different—and this one is tricky—God is more than one.

There is one God, but there are three persons in God.

GOD THE FATHER
GOD THE SON
GOD THE HOLY SPIRIT

Three persons in one God. I told you it was tricky.

And that is why God wasn't lonely. Because He wasn't alone.

There is love within God. There is friendship within God. There is family within God.

One day, God decided He wanted to make a **UNIVERSE**. He said, "It's time for us to begin." And **BOOM**! He started making stuff. *Why?* Because it made Him happy.

God made shining stars and the big, burning sun. He spun galaxies and solar systems and planets.

Then He picked one particular planet and said, "Watch this!" And **BOOM**! He made mountains and oceans and lakes and streams. He made plants grow—tiny little leafy ones smaller than a pebble, and big giant ones that climbed toward the sun.

It was very good. But God wasn't done.

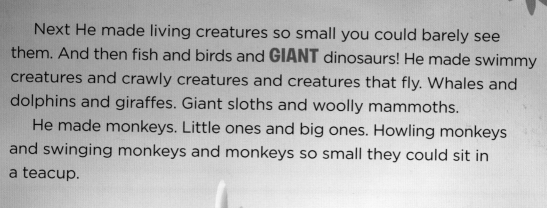

Next He made living creatures so small you could barely see them. And then fish and birds and **GIANT** dinosaurs! He made swimmy creatures and crawly creatures and creatures that fly. Whales and dolphins and giraffes. Giant sloths and woolly mammoths.

He made monkeys. Little ones and big ones. Howling monkeys and swinging monkeys and monkeys so small they could sit in a teacup.

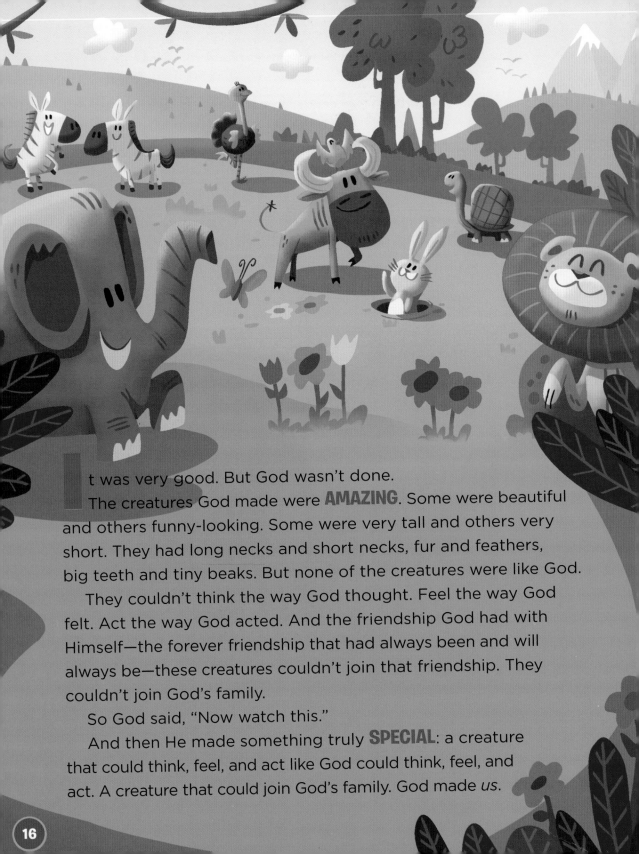

It was very good. But God wasn't done.

The creatures God made were **AMAZING**. Some were beautiful and others funny-looking. Some were very tall and others very short. They had long necks and short necks, fur and feathers, big teeth and tiny beaks. But none of the creatures were like God.

They couldn't think the way God thought. Feel the way God felt. Act the way God acted. And the friendship God had with Himself—the forever friendship that had always been and will always be—these creatures couldn't join that friendship. They couldn't join God's family.

So God said, "Now watch this."

And then He made something truly **SPECIAL**: a creature that could think, feel, and act like God could think, feel, and act. A creature that could join God's family. God made *us*.

CREATION
FAMILY CONNECTION

GENESIS 1

TRICKY BITS

How can God be one God, but three persons?

FATHER SON

HOLY SPIRIT

Each person is God, yet each is separate. *Tricky, right?* Just as a person is one person with different roles, the one true God is God, yet He impacts our lives as Father (God), Son (Jesus), and Holy Spirit (our Helper).

TALK

What does the creation story teach us about God's power?

What is your favorite part of God's creation?

Dear God . . .

PRAY

Dear God, thank You for creating our great, big world and for creating us to be a part of Your family. Amen.

ADAM
AND
EVE

Man and woman.

God made them, these very special creatures.

The man He named "Adam," and the woman He named "Eve." They were more like God than anything else God had made. They were humans and could **THINK** and **FEEL**. They could dream up big ideas and create things.

And most important, they could be friends with God.

The earth was a pretty wild place, so God planted a garden for Adam and Eve to live in. He called it "Eden."

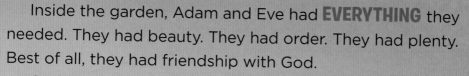

Inside the garden, Adam and Eve had **EVERYTHING** they needed. They had beauty. They had order. They had plenty. Best of all, they had friendship with God.

God gave Adam and Eve a great, amazing, and huge job: Take the beauty, order, and plenty of the garden, and spread it **EVERYWHERE**. Make the whole earth like the garden. And have kids. Lots of them! So, God's family could get bigger and bigger. So, love and joy and friendship and beauty and order and plenty could fill the whole earth! What a great, amazing, and **HUGE** job!

Of course, friendship needs trust. If Adam and Eve wanted to be God's friends, they needed to trust Him. They needed to listen to God.

That would be easy, right? If God is good and powerful and never wrong, trusting Him should be easy.

And it was . . . for a while.

But there was this **ONE** tree.

There were **LOTS** of trees in the garden, of course, and many were covered with fruit. Apple trees and pear trees and orange trees and lemon trees and apricot trees—more fruit than Adam and Eve could possibly eat!

But there was **ONE** particular tree in the garden that was different. God said, "Don't eat the fruit from **THAT** tree."

Just **ONE** tree. A gazillion trees with fruit they could eat, and just **ONE** tree they couldn't touch.

Would they listen to God? Would they stay away from that one tree? What would ***YOU*** *do?*

Well, Adam and Eve were doing just fine listening to God until a new voice showed up in the garden. This voice belonged to an enemy of God and was coming from a **SNAKE**. A sneaky snake.

The snake said, "Are you **SURE** you can't eat the fruit of that tree?"

Adam and Eve said they were sure. And that if they ate **THAT** fruit, they would die.

And then the snake did something that no one had ever done before in God's beautiful world.

The snake **LIED**.

"You will surely not die," he said. "No, if you eat the fruit of **THAT** tree, you will become wise and smart like God!"

Whoa. *What should Adam and Eve do? It would be great to be as wise as God! Then they wouldn't have to listen to God all the time—they'd know everything too!*

Who should they trust? The sneaky snake? Or God? Who would **YOU** *trust?*

Adam and Eve decided to trust the snake and go their own way. Adam and Eve ate the fruit they weren't supposed to eat. And **SIN** entered God's world.

ADAM AND EVE
FAMILY CONNECTION

GENESIS 2

FUN FACTS

Eden comes from a Hebrew word which is thought to mean "pleasure" or "delight." It's no wonder God's perfect garden was given this beautiful name! Experts say the garden of Eden likely occupied the land that is now the southeast tip of Iraq on the Persian Gulf.

TALK

Why did Adam and Eve want to eat the fruit God said they couldn't have?

What happens when we disobey God and go our own way?

Dear God . . .

PRAY

Dear God, help us to listen only to Your voice so that we go Your way instead of our own. Amen.

What's sin, you ask?

Sin is when we ignore God. When we go our own way. When we put ourselves first in front of our friends and neighbors—even in front of God! Sin is when we say to God, "I don't care what You say—I'm going to do it **MY** way!"

When sin entered God's world, everything changed. *Why?*

Since God is all good and sin is all bad, sin can't be close to God.

That sneaky snake knew this. He was trying to hurt God, and he knew that if he could get Adam and Eve to sin, then **THEY** couldn't be close to God! God's very favorite creatures—the only ones who could be His friends and join His family—would have to live their lives away from Him!

Because of their sin, Adam and Eve had to leave the garden. They couldn't be God's friends anymore. Adam and Eve would have to live in a wild world all by themselves.

The beauty, order, and plenty of the garden were no longer a part of Adam and Eve's life. The love and friendship and joy of being in God's family were lost.

God was very sad to see Adam and Eve living apart from Him as a result of their sin. He was very sad to see sin spread to their kids, and then **THEIR** kids, and then **THEIR** kids! All of God's favorite creatures were separated from Him.

But God had a plan.

It was a **RESCUE** plan: the kind of plan you need when someone is in big, **BIG** trouble. Sin and the sneaky snake had really messed up God's world. But God had a plan to fix it— to make things right. To save Adam and Eve and their kids, and their kids' kids, and their kids' kids' kids . . . all the way down to us!

What does God want to save us from? Three things.

First, He wants to save us from the **STAIN** of sin. Sin can't be close to God, and when we have the mark of sin on us, we can't be close to God either. God wants to "wash" the stain of sin off of us so we can be close to Him again.

Second, God wants to save us from the **POWER** of sin. Sin has a way of whispering in our ears to get us to sin even more. The more we sin, the easier it is to keep on sinning, and soon, sin takes over our lives!

But God can give us greater power to ignore the whispers of sin and live with peace and joy and love, which is **WAY** better than sin!

And third, even if God has saved us from the **STAIN** of sin and the **POWER** of sin, we still live in a world **FILLED** with sin. A world filled with tears and hurt, selfishness and meanness. God wants to save us from the **PRESENCE** of sin. When the time is right, God will make a world where His family can live in beauty and order and plenty—the way it was meant to be!

God looked down at the world and saw that sin was spreading. His beautiful world was drowning in sin! God knew there was only one way to stop His world from drowning in sin.

DROWN the sin.

WHAT IS SIN?
FAMILY CONNECTION

GENESIS 4:7

EVERYDAY TRUTH

God gives me the power to ignore the whispers of sin and choose His way!

TALK

Why does sin separate us from God?

What three things does God want to save us from?

Dear God . . .

PRAY

Dear God, thank You for saving us from sin so that we can be close to You. Amen.

NOAH AND THE FLOOD

Adam and Eve had kids. And their kids had kids. And their kids had kids. Grandkids and great-grandkids and great-great-grandkids—spreading all over the wild world. And **SIN** was spreading with them.

They were fighting. Stealing. Lying. Hurting each other. Making God's world an ugly place.

Finally, God said, "Enough!"

It was time to start again. God decided to pick one person—one good person—to start His world over again.

*But who? In all that sinning and fighting and hurting, was **ANYONE** good and kind enough to trust with such an important job?*

Yes!

God chose Noah. Noah was a righteous man— he tried very hard to make the right choices. He tried hard not to fight or steal or lie.

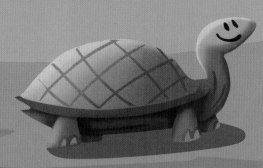

Noah walked with God. That means that, in a world where everyone was doing their own thing, Noah was thinking about God. Talking to God. Listening to God. Noah was always ready to do what God asked.

Oh, yeah—and there's one other thing we know about Noah. He was more than 500 years old. Yep, 500 years old. People lived a long time back then.

Not only was Noah a righteous man who walked with God, but Noah had been practicing walking with God—and listening for God's voice—for more than **500 YEARS**! That's a **LONG** time!

So when God had a really big job to do, He knew who to call because He knew who had been listening. **FOR MORE THAN 500 YEARS!!**

God said, "Hey Noah. Build a boat."

And Noah said, "What's a boat?"

And God said, "It's a thing you can float in if there's a flood."

And Noah said, "What's a flood?"

And God said, "It's when water covers everything. It's why you need a boat."

And Noah said, "How big?"

And God said, "Big enough for your family."

And Noah said, "Anything else?"

And God said, "And some animals."

And Noah said, "How many animals?"

And God said, "All of them."

At this point Noah probably fainted, and God probably had to poke him with a stick to wake him up again. Then God gave him plans for building a boat.

A very, very **BIG** boat.

Noah and his family set to work building a boat **SO BIG** it could hold all of them, plus two of every kind of animal!

Building a boat that big took years and years, and Noah's neighbors probably came by often to laugh at him for building a boat where there was no water.

But Noah didn't care about the laughing. He'd been walking with God for a long time, and he was going to keep on walking with God no matter what. Noah wanted to be God's friend, even if everyone else thought he was silly.

Then one day, it started to **RAIN**.

The animals came from **EVERYWHERE**. Big animals, little animals, tall animals, and short animals. God sent the animals to Noah, and Noah packed them all in his big, big boat.

And it kept raining. Harder and **HARDER**. Suddenly, having a boat looked like a pretty good idea.

God covered the land with water, so that all the sinning and fighting and hurting could finally stop. All the fighting and hurting died. But so did most of God's creation.

It was a very sad time.

It rained and poured for **40 DAYS**. Noah's big, big boat floated on the water . . . 50 days . . . 60 days . . . 100 days! After 150 days, the big, big boat was getting very, very **STINKY**! *Have you ever been on a pig farm or in the elephant house at the zoo?* Stinky like that—only worse!

Then finally, the water started to go down. Down, down, down . . . One day, at long last, Noah's big, big boat came to rest on top of a mountain.

"Let's start again," God said.

So Noah and his family—plus a whole bunch of seasick animals—walked out of the big, big boat into a clean, fresh world.

It was time to start again.

NOAH AND THE FLOOD
FAMILY CONNECTION

GENESIS 6

FUN FACTS

A *cubit* is a unit of measurement often used in biblical times. It measures approximately 1½ feet. The ark was 300 cubits long, 50 cubits wide, and 30 cubits high. That's big enough to hold one and a half football fields or two large airplanes!

TALK

Why did God save Noah and his family from the flood?

Why do you think Noah ignored those who laughed about his big boat?

Dear God . . .

PRAY

Dear God, thank You for being faithful to Noah because he was faithful to You. We want to be faithful to You too. Amen.

THE TOWER OF BABEL

It was a new start!

The great flood had stopped all the fighting and cheating and lying. Now Noah and his kids had a new chance to live as God's friends—the way they had always tried to live—sharing **LOVE** and **KINDNESS**, instead of meanness and hate.

The first thing Noah did was build an altar where he could give gifts to God. Noah gave gifts to God and thanked God for this new chance in a new world. God told Noah and his kids how He wanted them to live, and they promised they would do their best to live that way.

And it went pretty well. For a while. But . . .

Noah's kids had kids. And their kids had kids. And **THEIR** kids had kids. Grandkids and great-grandkids and great-great-grandkids.

They started building houses. And then they built a whole city! They were very proud of their city.

"What a great city we have built!" they said. "What else can we build?"

What if we built a tower? A tower that reached to the sky? Wouldn't that make us look strong?"

Building a city doesn't seem like a big deal. Building a tall tower doesn't seem like a big deal. But it **WAS** a big deal.

What they were really saying was this: "If we all live in one place, we can protect ourselves. We can feed ourselves. And a great tower will make us feel strong! Then we won't need a strong God. We will be the strong ones!"

Remember: God didn't want people to stay in one place. He wanted them to cover the whole world and make it like the **GARDEN** of **EDEN**—filled with beauty, order, and plenty. He wanted His special creatures—His friends—to rely on **HIM** for safety and food. He wanted them to trust in **HIS** strength, not their own. To build things together **WITH HIM**, not on their own.

So as these grandkids and great-grandkids of Noah began building their mighty tower to the sky, God did something interesting.

He scrambled their words.

God gave them different languages, so they couldn't understand each other!

If they couldn't understand each other, they couldn't work together to build their tower. They couldn't work together to continue building their big city.

And sure enough, since they couldn't understand each other, different groups and families wandered off from the city to live in different parts of the world. Just like God wanted.

Little cities sprouted up all over. The "great tower" never got built.

So . . . did all the people say they were sorry for trying to live without God? Did they trust in God again, stop sinning, and start spreading beauty, order, and plenty throughout the world?

Not exactly.

Wherever there were groups of people living together, there was sin. More fighting, more cheating, more lying, and more hurting.

Even with their second chance, the grandkids and great-grandkids of Noah made the same mistake that Adam and Eve had made long before.

They stopped listening to God and started listening to that other voice. The voice of the sneaky snake that said, "You won't be happy if God is in charge. **YOU** should be in charge instead!" A voice that lied.

God saw His favorite creatures hurting each other and wandering farther and farther from Him. So, God knew it was time for His **GREAT** rescue plan—a plan that didn't start with a huge flood or a big boat. A plan that started with one single person.

A guy named Abram.

THE TOWER OF BABEL
FAMILY CONNECTION

GENESIS 11:1-9

TRICKY BITS

Was the Tower of Babel where all languages started?

Because the people disobeyed, God scrambled their words. They couldn't understand each other! Some Bible leaders believe this is the origin of languages, which forced people to live in different parts of the world, just like God wanted.

TALK

Why was it a big deal for the people to build a tall, tall tower?

Why did God scramble their words?

Dear God . . .

PRAY

Dear God, help us quiet the voices that say we should trust our strength instead of Yours. We want everything we say and do to bring glory to You. Amen.

GOD CALLS ABRAM

Once again, the world was sinking in sin. People were fighting, cheating, lying, ignoring God, and hurting each other. It wasn't the way God wanted it to be.

And people were building bigger and bigger cities. One of the biggest was a city called "Ur." *Isn't that a great name?* Just two letters: **U-R**.

If someone asked you where you live, and you said, 'Ur,' they'd say, "No, really, where do you live?"

And you'd say, "Ur."

And they'd say, "Stop making that noise. Where do you live?"

That would be fun. But we don't have many cities with names like Ur today. We have Chicago, Birmingham, London, and Dubai. Oh, that one's kind of fun to say, but not as much fun as a name that sounds like your stomach growling. Urrr . . .

But back to our story.

There was a man living in Ur named **ABRAM**. You probably know of him as **ABRAHAM** because later on God changed his name. But before he was Abraham, he was Abram.

Abram lived in Ur with his **FAMILY**. And when I say "family," I don't mean his mom and dad. I mean his mom, dad, sisters, brothers, uncles, aunts, cousins, second cousins, third cousins . . . and on and on.

You see, in the ancient world you were safer if you were in a big group. You were less likely to be robbed or attacked by another group of people if your group of people was really big. Going out on your own in the ancient world was a **DANGEROUS** thing to do. So people didn't go out on their own. They stuck with their families.

One day, God showed up and said, "Hey Abram, I want you to go out on your **OWN**."

At this point, Abram didn't know much about God. He didn't have the Bible like we do, because it hadn't been written yet. He couldn't go to church like we can, because there weren't any churches yet. But Abram **TRUSTED** God.

So when God said to Abram, "Leave your family and follow Me," do you know what Abram said?

He said, "Okay."

I know. Crazy. *Why did Abram trust God when he didn't even know Him yet? Would* **YOU** *have trusted God if* **YOU** *were Abram?*

That's not all God said to Abram, though. God told Abram that if he did what God **ASKED**, Abram wouldn't be alone. God would be with him.

Not only that, but God would give him so many kids and grandkids and great-grandkids that Abram's family would become an entire nation! And they'd have their own land! And the **WHOLE WORLD** would be blessed—given an amazing gift—through Abram and his kids!

Wow.

So Abram said, "Okay."

He left his family. He left his country. He left everything behind and wandered off into the middle of nowhere, following a God he had just met.

He took his wife with him. Her name was **SARAI**. You probably know her as **SARAH**, because soon after, God would change her name too.

They didn't take any children with them, though, because they didn't have any children. Sarai and Abram really wanted to have children, but God hadn't blessed them with any.

Which might make you ask a very important question: *How was Abram supposed to build a big, big family that could be a whole nation if he didn't have any children?*

And **THAT'S** the story we'll tell **NEXT**!

GOD CALLS ABRAM
FAMILY CONNECTION

GENESIS 12, 15

EVERYDAY TRUTH

I follow God because He leads me the right way!

TALK

What three promises did God make to Abram?

How can you follow God's call like Abram did?

Dear God . . .

PRAY

Dear God, we want to follow where You lead us every day. Please show us which way to go. Amen.

ABRAHAM'S FAMILY

In the ancient world having kids was

very important. Lots of kids. *Why?* Because living in the ancient world took a lot of work. You needed people to plant and harvest grain. People to take care of sheep. People to take care of goats. People to take care of camels. If you were attacked by another group of people, you needed people to help fight back!

The **MORE** kids and grandkids you had, the **MORE** help you had in planting and harvesting and shepherding and protecting. The more kids and grandkids you had, the better your life would be.

Which is why it was so terrible that Abram and Sarai didn't have any kids. And why God's promise that Abram's family would become a nation was so exciting!

By now Abram and Sarai had been following God for twenty-four years. They had wandered all over the land God said would be theirs. They had wandered down to Egypt and back again. And God had blessed Abram—he now had lots of servants and sheep and goats and camels.

The only thing Abram and Sarai still didn't have was kids.

Abram was about to give up on the idea of building a family when God told him two things.

First, God said, "Your name isn't Abram anymore. It's **ABRAHAM**. And Sarai's name is now **SARAH**."

And Abraham said, "Okay."

Then God said, "And next year Sarah will have a **BABY**."

And do you know what Abraham did?

He laughed.

Why did he laugh? Because the next year Sarah would turn ninety years old. Abraham had never heard of a ninety-year-old woman having a baby. *Have* **YOU** *ever heard of a ninety-year-old woman having a baby?*

Abraham tried not to, but he couldn't help it. He laughed.

Then God said, "And the baby will be named **ISAAC**." Which means—get this—"he laughs."

Isn't that hilarious?

A year later Sarah had a baby boy, and they named him Isaac. Everyone was amazed at this God who could make promises and keep them. Even promises that sounded **CRAZY**.

God wanted to see if Abraham really trusted Him. Really, **REALLY** trusted Him. So when Isaac was older, God asked Abraham if he would give up his son.

Did Abraham really **TRUST** *God?*

This was the child they had waited for! The child God had promised. The child God would use to bless the whole world. *What if Isaac died? Would God still keep His promise? Would God bring Isaac back to life?*

Abraham didn't know for sure. But he did know one thing.

He **TRUSTED** God.

So Abraham got ready to give up Isaac, because God asked him to.

But God didn't want Isaac to die. He just wanted to know if Abraham trusted Him. As soon as Abraham was ready to give up Isaac, God sent an ANGEL, who called out to Abraham from heaven.

"Stop! Do not lay a hand on the boy."

Then something amazing happened.

God learned that Abraham would trust Him, no matter what. Abraham learned that God would keep His promises, no matter what.

Isaac learned that he could trust God just as much as his father did. He learned that he could trust God with his LIFE.

So God said, "Now I can use you to build My nation!"

ABRAHAM'S FAMILY
FAMILY CONNECTION

GENESIS 21-22

TRICKY BITS

What is a sacrifice?

To *sacrifice* means to "give up something." In the Bible, an animal sacrifice was often payment for sin. God didn't really want Abraham to sacrifice his son. He only wanted to know that Abraham trusted Him. *Did you see the ram?* Go back and look for it. God provided the ram so Abraham wouldn't have to sacrifice Issac.

TALK

What did Abraham learn because he trusted God, no matter what?

What is one way you can trust God right now?

Dear God . . .

PRAY

Dear God, help us to obey You the way Abraham did, even when we don't understand Your plan. Amen.

53

JOSEPH

Because Abraham trusted God, he became God's friend. Because Abraham's son Isaac trusted God, he became God's friend too.

Then Isaac had a son named Jacob, who—*you guessed it*—learned from his father to trust God. And then Jacob had a son. And then Jacob had another son. And another. And another.

Jacob had twelve sons in all! Their names were Reuben, Simeon, Levi, Judah, Dan, Naphtali, Gad, Asher, Issachar, Zebulun, Joseph, and Benjamin.

Of all Jacob's sons, **JOSEPH** was his favorite. Jacob wanted Joseph to know that he was his dad's favorite, so he gave Joseph a special coat made of all the colors of the rainbow. This annoyed his older brothers. *Why didn't **THEY** get special coats?*

To make matters worse, Joseph told his older brothers about dreams he was having. In his dreams, Joseph saw himself ruling over his brothers. He saw his brothers bowing down to him.

Hearing about Joseph's dreams made his older brothers **REALLY** annoyed and **REALLY** jealous. So much so that they decided they'd be happier if Joseph wasn't around anymore.

So one day when their dad wasn't with them, they picked Joseph up and threw him in a hole in the ground! They were just going to leave him there forever—until they got **ANOTHER** idea.

Have you ever gotten so mad at your brother or sister that you wanted to sell them to the circus? Well, Joseph's brothers actually did. Except not to the circus. They sold Joseph to some folks traveling to Egypt, who sold Joseph **AGAIN** when they got to Egypt.

Now Joseph has been thrown in a hole and sold **TWICE**! What a lousy week!

In Egypt, Joseph worked for a very wealthy man. Joseph was honest and hardworking, and the wealthy man liked him. But the man's wife told a lie about him and Joseph went to prison!

Now Joseph has been thrown in a hole, sold twice, **AND** sent to prison! *Why would God let all that happen to Jacob's favorite son? Wasn't Jacob a friend of God?*

Joseph could have gotten mad and decided he didn't want to be God's friend anymore. But he didn't. He still prayed to God and he still tried hard to do the right thing.

And God had a **PLAN** for Joseph.

While in prison, Joseph told two of the men there the meaning of their **CRAZY** dreams. God showed Joseph what the dreams meant.

A few years later, Pharaoh, the king of all Egypt, also had a crazy dream. He'd heard about a guy named Joseph who could interpret dreams. Pharaoh called Joseph out of prison and told him the dream. Once again, God gave Joseph the meaning.

The dream, Joseph said, was a **WARNING**. For seven years, Egypt would grow lots and lots of food. More than they could eat! But then for seven years after that, they would experience a famine—when no food would grow at all. If the Egyptians didn't store up all the extra food during the first seven years, they wouldn't have enough to eat during the famine, and many people would **DIE**!

Pharaoh was so happy that he made Joseph the second-most powerful person in Egypt and put him in charge of all the food. Joseph made sure they would have enough to eat when things got tough.

When food stopped growing in Egypt, it also stopped growing where Joseph's family lived. They were really hungry! **SO** hungry that they traveled all the way to Egypt to see if they could find food there.

And sure enough—not only did they find plenty of food in Egypt, but they **ALSO** found their brother Joseph! They thought Joseph would be mad at them, but he wasn't.

Why wasn't Joseph mad?

Because he could see God's plan. If Joseph hadn't been thrown in a hole, sold twice, and then sent to prison, Egypt would have run out of food and many, many people would have died. Joseph's family would have run out of food and **THEY** would have died! God used something very bad—the way his brothers treated him—to do something very good—to save Joseph's whole family!

Joseph learned that God can use anything, no matter how bad, to do something **GOOD**.

JOSEPH
FAMILY CONNECTION

GENESIS 37

EVERYDAY TRUTH

When I trust God, He uses the hard parts of my story for my good and His glory.

TALK

Why wasn't Joseph mad at his brothers for selling him to be a slave in Egypt?

What can God do with the bad things that happen to us?

Dear God . . .

PRAY

Dear God, we believe You can use our hard days to do something good. Help us to stay positive as we trust You. Amen.

MOSES IS BORN

Joseph and his brothers were in Egypt. Everyone was all right, and they had enough food, which was great. *But which of God's promises had come true?*

Had Abraham's family become a great nation? Nope. Abraham and Sarah had a son and all of his kids and their kids numbered about seventy people. That's a big family, but it's not a whole "nation."

Did they have their own land? Nope. They were living in Egypt, someone else's land.

Had they blessed the "whole world"? They didn't even know what that promise meant. *How does one family "bless the whole world"?*

Of the three big promises given to Abraham, at that point a total of **ZERO** had come true.

Well, Jacob's sons had kids. And their kids had kids. And **THEIR** kids had kids. A lot of kids! There were hundreds of kids. And then **THOUSANDS** of kids!

Then the Pharaoh who was Joseph's friend died, and there was a new Pharaoh. And then a new Pharaoh after that. And pretty soon Egypt was being ruled by a Pharaoh who didn't know **ANYTHING** about Joseph. He just knew that there were thousands and thousands of these people running around—these "children of Israel."

Remember how God changed Abram's name to Abraham, and Sarai's name to Sarah? Well, God also changed Jacob's name—to Israel. So, all of Jacob's children—and his grandchildren, and his great-grandchildren—became the "children of Israel." They were also called "Israelites."

Now the new Pharaoh said, "Hey! There are too many Israelites around here!" And he decided to do something about it.

First, he made the Israelites **SLAVES** to the Egyptians. A *slave* is "a person who is owned by another person." A slave had to do whatever his or her owner said. Being slaves meant the children of Israel had to do whatever Pharaoh said. They had to build stuff. And farm stuff. And clean stuff.

Being slaves also meant they couldn't leave Egypt. Ever. Which was a big problem, if you remember God's second promise—that His people would have their own land. *How can you have your own land if you can't ever leave someone else's?*

But it got **WORSE**. The children of Israel kept having more kids. More and more kids! Eventually there were so many babies that Pharaoh decided to do something really bad: get rid of the Israelites! Every Israelite baby boy, he said, should be thrown into the river.

Then God gave one Israelite woman an **IDEA**. When her baby boy was young, she made a basket that floated like a boat and put her baby inside. Then she hid the basket in the tall grass at the edge of the river and waited to see what **GOD** would do next.

A group of Egyptian girls were washing at the river and they noticed the basket. They opened it up and—**WHAT?**—there was a baby . . .

One of the girls decided that she would take him home and raise him as her own son. *Can you guess who that girl was?*

It was Pharaoh's daughter! The daughter of the king of Egypt! Pharaoh's daughter brought home an Israelite baby to live in the palace just like an Egyptian—and right next to Pharaoh!

She gave the baby a name—MOSES—and he was about to become a very big part of God's rescue plan!

EXODUS 2

TRICKY BITS

If slavery is wrong, why does it happen so often in the Bible?

Many of the things that happened in the Bible went against God's heart for people. Remember, when Adam and Eve first sinned, God's world got turned upside down. Today, we understand that owning another person is wrong. We should continue to pray and fight for those who are mistreated.

TALK

Why did Moses' mom put him in a basket in the river?

Why do you think it was important for God to save Moses?

Dear God . . .

PRAY

Dear God, thank You for showing us what to do when we face the impossible. Amen.

THE BURNING BUSH

Moses grew up in Pharaoh's

palace as if he were Egyptian, even though he knew he wasn't. He knew he was really a child of Israel. An **ISRAELITE**.

One day Moses saw an Egyptian man hitting an Israelite worker. This made Moses really mad, because he was an Israelite too! He got **SO** mad that he, well . . . he killed the Egyptian.

Yep. He got a little **TOO** mad! *Have you ever made a mistake because you were just **SO** mad?* Yeah. That's what happened to Moses.

Moses knew he was in big trouble, so he ran off into the desert to hide.

For **40 YEARS**.

That's a **LONG** time to hide. But he was sure if he came back to Egypt, Pharaoh would find him and kill him. So, he stayed in the desert.

Moses hid in the desert for so long he eventually met a nice girl named **ZIPPORAH**, got married, had kids, and became a shepherd. His new life was much better than getting killed by Pharaoh, so Moses figured he'd just stay in the desert and never go back to Egypt. Ever. No matter what.

Until one day . . .

One day, when Moses was minding his own business (and his sheep) in the desert, he saw something weird. A bush was burning, but it didn't burn up. It just kept burning. And burning.

That's weird, he thought.

And then the bush **SAID** something.

Well, it wasn't really the bush talking. It was God . . . talking **THROUGH** the bush that was burning.

Since this was not a normal thing for Moses—or *anyone,* for that matter—he decided he'd better listen.

"Hey Moses," said God. "The children of Israel are having a terrible time in Egypt. I've heard them crying, and it is time to **SAVE** them and bring them to the land I promised."

"That's great!" answered Moses.

Then God said, "I want you to do it. You're going to go to Pharaoh and tell him to let the Israelites leave."

And Moses said, "That's a **TERRIBLE** idea!"

Moses explained that he wasn't very popular in Egypt. After all, he had killed a guy.

And God said, "I'll come with you."

Moses went on to say that he really didn't like public speaking, and that maybe someone else would be better for the job.

Again, God said, "I'll come with you."

Moses asked why Pharaoh would even listen to him if he just showed up and said, "Let my people go!"

And once again God said, "I'll come with you."

Then, as if the burning bush weren't impressive enough, God turned Moses' walking stick into a scary SNAKE, and then back into a stick, because, well, He's God and He can do things like that.

So after he stopped running from the scary stick-snake, Moses asked, "Would You do cool stuff like that in front of Pharaoh?"

God replied, "And stuff even MORE amazing than that."

Moses thought and thought and thought, and finally said, "Okay. I'll go back to Egypt. And You'll come with me, right?"

And then God probably said, "What part of 'I'll come with you' don't you understand?"

So, very nervously, Moses and his family started walking back to Egypt.

And God went with him.

THE BURNING BUSH
FAMILY CONNECTION

EXODUS 3-4

EVERYDAY TRUTH

I can do hard things because God is always with me!

TALK

Dear God . . .

Why did Moses think he was a terrible choice to rescue God's people from Egypt?

When have you needed to trust God because you were afraid?

PRAY

Dear God, help us remember that when You ask us to do something big, You always help us! Amen.

LET MY PEOPLE GO!

Let my people go."
That's what Moses said as he stood in front of Pharaoh. He was probably very nervous. He didn't want to be in Egypt. He wanted to be back home in the desert, with his sheep and his wife and his kids.

But there he was! Standing in front of Pharaoh, saying exactly what God had told him to say.

"Let my people go!"

And do you know what Pharaoh said?

He said, "No."

Rats. Okay . . . it was time for that neat trick with the scary stick-snake. So, Moses threw down his walking stick, and—**BOOM!**—God turned it into a snake, and back into a stick.

"Let my people go!" he said again.

And Pharaoh said, "No."

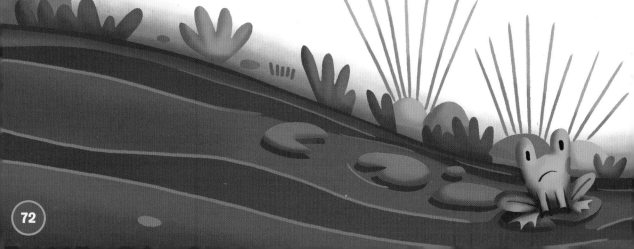

Double rats. Then God told Moses it was time to do something even **MORE** powerful than the stick-snake. So, He began to send plagues, one at a time, to show Pharaoh just how powerful He was. A "plague" is a really **BAD** thing—like bugs or a bad rash or a really big storm—stuff you don't want happening in your town.

God told Moses to dip his walking stick in the big river in Egypt, called the Nile. When his stick touched the river, all the water turned to **BLOOD**!

"Let my people go!" Moses said once again.

And Pharaoh said, "No."

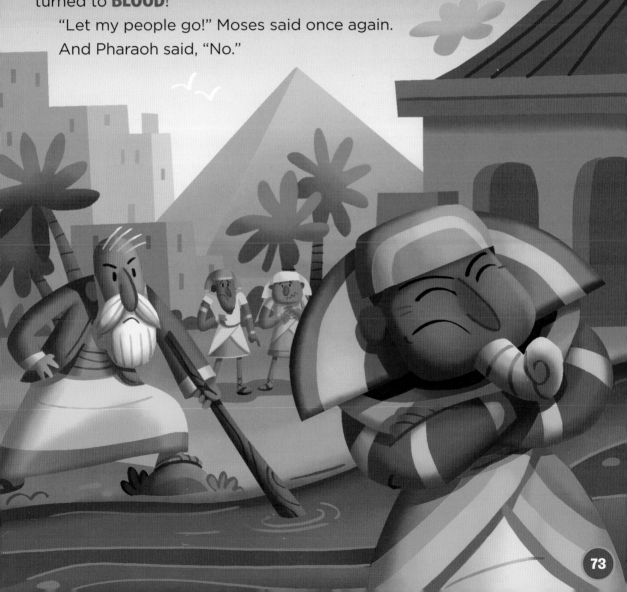

Then God said to Moses, "Hold up your stick. We're going to make frogs."

And **BOOM**! Frogs. **MILLIONS** of them! **EVERYWHERE**. The fields were covered with frogs. The roads were covered with frogs. There were frogs in people's houses. Even in their beds!

"Let my people go!" Moses said, trying not to step on a frog. And Pharaoh said, "No."

Next God sent gnats—tiny little bugs that got **EVERYWHERE**. Then flies! Zillions of flies! And then a sickness that killed all the farm animals. Next, all the Egyptians got sores on their skin. Itchy, ouchy sores all over!

There was **HAIL**! Big balls of ice that fell from the sky and knocked down all the corn and wheat and rice plants. And then **LOCUSTS**, big bugs that look like grasshoppers and ate all the crops that weren't killed by the hail!

Each time, Pharaoh said, "No."

These plagues—the frogs and flies and locusts and hail—weren't enough, so God turned out the lights.

Egypt actually went **DARK**. It was middle-of-the-night dark in the middle of the day. The Egyptians couldn't see anything.

"Let my people go!" Moses said to Pharaoh. At least he thought he was talking to Pharaoh. It was so dark it was hard to tell.

But a voice from the darkness said . . . "No."

Finally, God knew exactly what He would have to do to change Pharaoh's mind.

God told Moses it was time for the Egyptians to know how **POWERFUL** He was. "I am going to send an angel who will kill all the oldest sons of the Egyptians," He said. "And then Pharaoh will let My people go."

Moses thought hard about this terrible thing.

"How will the angel know which sons are the children of Israel?" Moses asked.

God gave Moses a **SIGN**. Each Israelite family was to prepare a lamb for a special meal, and then take some of the blood of that lamb and put it over the door of their house. When the angel saw the blood of the lamb over the door, the angel would pass over that house.

Moses and the Israelites were unsure, but they followed God's directions. They put the blood of the lamb over their doors. They ate the special meal, which is now called **PASSOVER**. They did everything just the way God had said, and then they went to bed. But they didn't get much sleep.

That night an angel passed through all the streets of Egypt. And in the morning, all of the oldest sons of the Egyptians were dead.

The Egyptian moms and dads cried and cried. Even Pharaoh cried, because his son died too.

It was terrible.

When he was done crying, Pharaoh called for Moses.

Can you guess what he said?

He said, "Go."

God showed the Egyptians just how powerful He was. He showed the children of Israel that He heard their cries and that He would keep the promises He had made to their father Abraham.

But that's not all.

God also gave a hint about His third promise . . . the blessing for the whole world. Someday all of God's children would be saved from death. All it would take would be the blood of a very, very special Lamb.

LET MY PEOPLE GO!
FAMILY CONNECTION

FUN FACTS

The Passover meal, shared to remember this important event, consists of six symbolic items:

- *Maror* and *chazeret*, bitter herbs and romaine lettuce, representing the bitterness of slavery in Egypt
- *Charoses*, a sweet paste of fruit and nuts, representing the mortar used by the slaves to build in Egypt
- *Karpas*, a vegetable, such as celery, symbolizing hope, dipped in salt water to represent the tears shed by the Israelites
- *Zeroah*, a roasted lamb, representing the sacrifice
- *Beitzah*, a roasted egg, a symbol of life

TALK

Can you name all ten plagues?

What did the plagues show the Egyptians and the Israelites about God?

Dear God . . .

PRAY

Dear God, thank You for always protecting us by Your great power. Amen.

77

THE TEN COMMANDMENTS

After 400 years in Egypt, the Israelites were finally free! *Can you imagine how that would feel?*

It wasn't easy. Immediately they ran into trouble, and immediately God showed up to help.

The Red Sea was in the way of their escape! So, God pushed the water aside and they walked right through.

They had no food to eat! So, God sent birds for meat and weird, flaky stuff called manna for bread.

They had no water to drink! So, God told Moses to hit a rock with his walking stick and—**BOOM**! A fountain of water came right out of the rock.

But even though God was with them—giving them everything they needed—the children of Israel still complained.

"IT'S TOO HOT."
"WE'RE THIRSTY."
"WE'RE TIRED OF EATING THIS WEIRD FLAKY STUFF."

Where was this new land? Why did they have to be in the desert? How long would they have to keep walking?

God wanted more than just to get them to the land He had promised. He wanted to make them a nation whose king was God Himself! The Israelites needed more than just directions for where to go—they needed directions for how to live. They needed to understand how to be a nation ruled by God.

You see, even though they were the children of Israel, they still sinned. Sometimes they were mean. Sometimes they would put themselves first. And remember, people who sin can't be close to God.

So how could sinful people live with God as their king? It was going to be hard.

It was going to take work.

It was going to take **RULES**.

LOTS and **LOTS** of rules.

God led Moses up a mountain called Mount Sinai, so they could talk about these rules, and He started out by giving Moses ten really important ones—so important that He carved them into big stone tablets! They were so important that today they have their own name: the Ten Commandments.

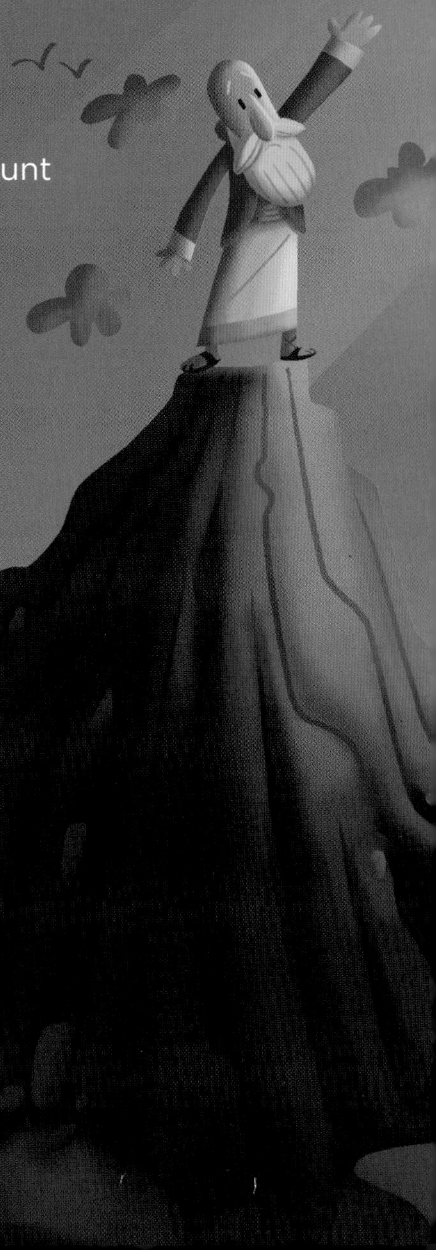

"You must not have any other gods except Me."

This was a big one. Egypt had lots of pretend gods, and some of the Israelites had started worshipping those gods instead of the true God. God made it clear that He was the only god they should bow down to.

"Do not make any idols."

In the ancient world, an idol was usually a small statue that stood for a god. People would pray to and give offerings to these statues. "None of that!" God said.

"Be careful how you use My name."

God's name deserves respect. The Israelites were to use God's name seriously—and only when they were talking about Him.

"Remember the Sabbath day."

God wanted the Israelites to take one day each week and give that day to Him as a reminder that everything they had was from God.

"Honor your father and mother."

Respect your mom and dad. Listen to them. And take care of them when they're old and can't take care of themselves. This makes God happy.

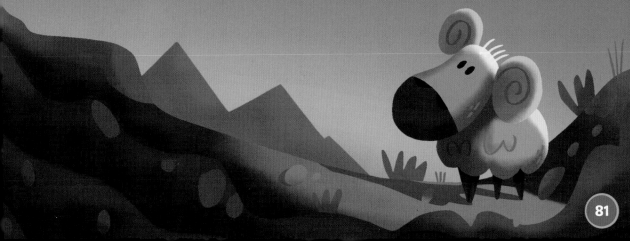

"Do not murder anyone."

There was a lot of murder in the ancient world. But God didn't want murder in His nation.

"Do not be guilty of adultery."

Adultery is when you take someone else's wife or husband and act like they're your wife or husband. It's sort of like stealing, and it breaks up families, which are very important to God.

"Do not steal."

Speaking of stealing . . . don't take things that don't belong to you.

"Do not tell lies."

Be honest. Don't try to get yourself out of trouble—or get other people into trouble—by saying things that aren't true.

"Do not covet."

Covet means "to want to take." If you covet someone's bike, it means you want to take his bike. God says to be happy with what you have. Don't desire to take the things other people have.

Ten big rules carved in stone! *But was that everything the Israelites needed to do to live with God as their king?* Not even close. Moses was about to learn that the Ten Commandments weren't the end of God's rules for Israel. They were just the **BEGINNING**.

THE TEN COMMANDMENTS
FAMILY CONNECTION

EVERYDAY TRUTH

God's guidance shows me where to go. God's guidelines show me how to live.

TALK

Why was it important for God's people to have rules?

If directions tell you where to go, what do rules tell you?

Dear God . . .

PRAY

Dear God, thank You for giving us guidelines for how to live in a way that honors You. Amen.

LAWS, LAWS, LAWS

Have you ever heard the word HOLY? It's an important word in the Bible, and many people don't understand what it really means. Lots of people think the word HOLY means "better than."

But that isn't what it means at all. *Holy* doesn't mean "better than." It means "different from."

Specifically, the word *holy* means "set apart for God."

When we say that something is "holy," it means that it has been set apart to be used only for God. When a person is holy, that person has been set apart for God.

So what do we mean when we say God is holy? That God has been set apart . . . for God? That doesn't really make any sense.

No, when we say God is holy, we mean God is set apart from **EVERYTHING**. God is completely different from anyone or anything. There is no one like God. Anywhere.

As Moses led the Israelites through the desert, God was forming them into a nation. He wanted this nation to be holy— to be set apart for Him. This was the kingdom of God, and it was a **REAL** kingdom in a **REAL** place, with people, walls, houses, horses, farms . . . everything needed to be a new nation.

But if Israel was going to be a real nation, Israel needed lots of laws. So God gave Moses laws for how they should treat each other, for buying and selling land, for loaning and borrowing money, for worshipping Him, and for giving money or animals or crops as a sacrifice or payment for their sin.

God also gave Israel laws about the food they could eat. And the clothes they could wear. Even about their hair and their beards! That's right—God's people had **BEARD** laws!

And this is where things can get a little confusing for us today. When you read all the laws God gave to Moses, you might notice something—we still follow many of those laws today. But many others we do not.

Why is that? Aren't all of God's laws good for us to follow?

For example, God told the Israelites not to murder, lie, or steal. And today, we still believe it is wrong to murder, lie, or steal.

But God also told the Israelites not to eat any meat that comes from a pig. He told them to put little dangly tassels on the corners of their coats. He told the Israelite men to never, ever trim their beards. Just let them **GROW** and **GROW** and **GROW**.

Today we don't follow those rules. We eat bacon and ham, which come from pigs. We don't put tassels on our coats. And **EXCEPT** for hipsters and lumberjacks, we usually don't let our beards grow and grow and grow. We shave them right off if we want to!

To understand why we follow some of Israel's laws but not others, we need to understand the three different kinds of laws God gave to Israel.

First, God gave Israel **CIVIL** laws. *Civil laws* are laws for running a city or country. Laws about governments and armies and taxes. Laws about buying and selling houses and land. Because we don't live in Israel, we don't follow Israel's civil laws. We follow the civil laws of the nations we live in today.

God also gave Israel **RITUAL** laws. A *ritual* is "an action you do over and over as a symbol of something you believe." Remember, God wanted the Israelites to be *holy*—to be set apart for Him. So God gave them rules about the food they ate, the clothes they wore, even how to grow their beards and hair. He gave them rules about special days and special feasts. All of these things reminded the Israelites every day that they were different from the nations around them. They were a nation **SET APART** for God.

Today, God isn't setting apart a nation for Himself like Israel, so he doesn't ask us to follow Israel's ritual laws.

And finally, God gave Israel **ETHICAL** laws. *Ethical* means "how we act," so *ethical laws* are laws about how we treat each other. Laws about lying and stealing and murdering. About wanting things that don't belong to us. These are ethical laws, and they weren't just for Israel. They're for all of us. Everywhere. All the time.

That's why today, God doesn't mind if we eat bacon.

Unless it's someone else's bacon.

LAWS, LAWS, LAWS
FAMILY CONNECTION

TRICKY BITS

Why do we follow some of the laws in the Bible but not all of them?
To understand why, look at the types of laws God gave to Israel:

TYPE OF LAW	BASED ON . . .	TODAY . . .
Civil Laws	the government we live in	we follow the laws of our government *(laws about taxes, land, and houses)*
Ritual Laws	the culture of the day	we observe some rituals to honor God's story *(laws about food, clothes, and holidays)*
Ethical Laws	moral right and wrong	we still live God's way, choosing what is right *(laws about stealing, lying, hurting people)*

TALK

What does it mean to be *holy?*

What are the three types of laws explained in the Bible?

Dear God . . .

PRAY

Dear God, we want to be set apart for You. Please show us how to live Your way every day. Amen.

TIME-OUT!

Have you ever been put in time-out?

Maybe for not listening to your mom or dad? Or being mean to your sister or brother?

Well, **YOUR** time-out was nothing compared to Israel's time-out. God put Israel in time-out for **40 YEARS**!

What did they do to get a forty-year time-out? Well, Moses and the Israelites had lots of new rules from God about how to be His holy nation. They knew what to do and what not to do. No beard trimming, no pork eating, no lying or stealing . . . lots of rules.

As soon as they left camp to head for the Promised Land, the Israelites started complaining again.

"IT'S TOO HOT!"
"WE'RE TIRED OF THIS WEIRD, FLAKY FOOD!"

They were complaining about **EVERYTHING**. Moses told them to trust God and be patient. After all, they were headed to the land God had promised them. They would soon have their own land and be God's holy nation!

Just when Moses thought he couldn't take their complaining any longer, they finally reached the Promised Land—a land called Canaan.

There was one small problem though. There were already people living in Canaan.

So Moses sent **TWELVE** spies into the land to check it out. *Do you know what a spy is?* It's someone who sneaks around gathering information without being noticed. The twelve spies wandered all over Canaan, taking notes. *Was there food? Fresh water? Were there trees? How many people lived there? Were they big people? Or little people?*

Then they came back to Moses and the Israelites and told them what they saw. The Promised Land was amazing! They saw grapes—**HUGE**, delicious grapes. They saw lots of fruit trees. They saw good land for growing crops, with clean, fresh water running in brooks and streams!

They saw that the land God promised them was an amazing, wonderful place to live.

BUT . . .

They also saw the people who lived there. They looked big. They looked strong. They looked mean. *What if they attacked the Israelites? Would the Israelites win or lose?*

Moses asked the spies what the Israelites should do.

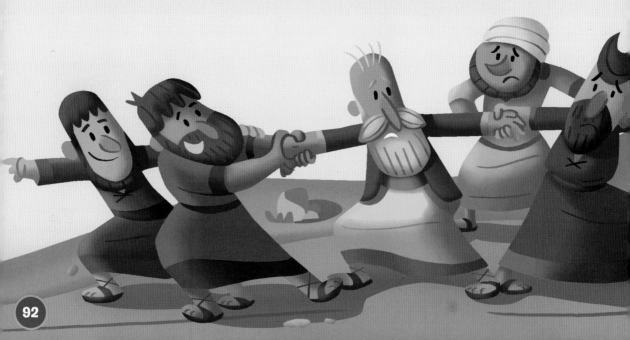

Two of the spies reminded the Israelites that this was the land God promised. Even though the people there looked big, God was **BIGGER**! If they had to fight for the land, God would fight with them, and they would **WIN**! All they had to do was trust God.

But the other ten spies were scared. "The people are too big!" they said. "They're too strong!" they said. "If we have to fight them, we'll lose!"

*Who should the Israelites listen to? The two spies who trusted God? Or the ten spies who were so scared they wanted to run away? Who would **YOU** listen to?*

The Israelites listened to the scared spies. They forgot all the things God had done to bring them out of Egypt. They forgot that He was always with them and that He was bigger than anyone or anything they could ever face!

They **FORGOT** about God.

They said, "We're not going into that land. Let's go back to Egypt!" Moses couldn't believe what he was hearing. The children of Israel—God's friends—were turning their backs on God.

"Because you don't trust Me, none of you will go into the land I promised," God said. "Someday, your children will go in, but you won't."

God wanted the Israelites to trust Him. He wanted them to remember that He loved them very much, and that they didn't need to be afraid, because He was **ALWAYS** with them!

The Israelites forgot all of these things.

And so, God put them in time-out . . . for forty years.

TIME-OUT!
FAMILY CONNECTION

FUN FACTS

During their forty-year time-out, Moses and the Israelites wandered the desert in the Sinai Peninsula—which is situated between the Mediterranean and the Red seas. Today, the location of the Israelites' wilderness wandering is a 23,000-square-mile bridge between Africa and Asia, with a population of almost 1.5 million people.

TALK

Why did God's people get a forty-year time-out?

What can we remember about God when we encounter hard things?

Dear God . . .

PRAY

Dear God, thank You for being bigger and stronger than our fears. We trust You to help us bravely through. Amen.

FROM EGYPT TO THE PROMISED LAND

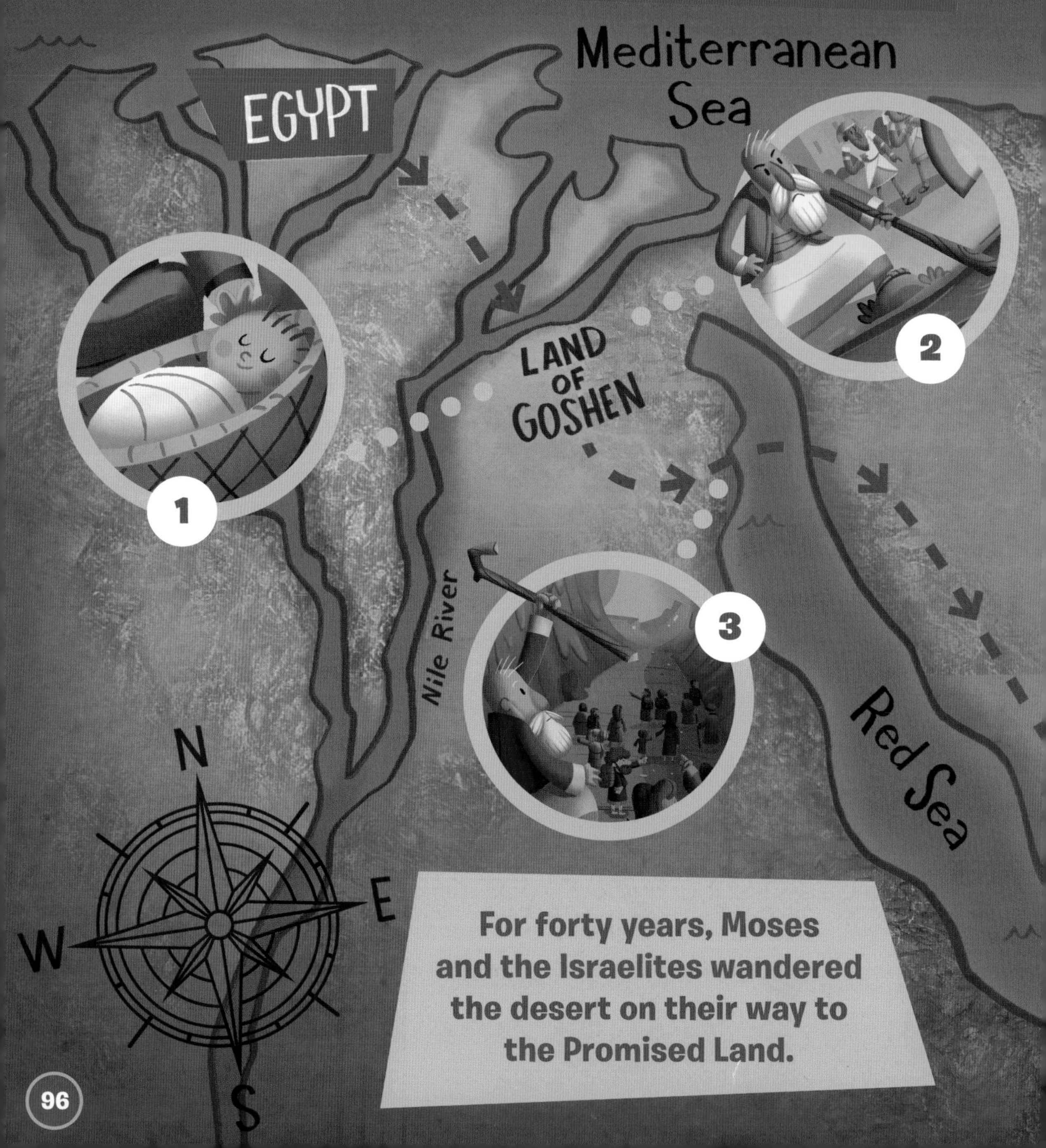

EGYPT

Mediterranean Sea

LAND OF GOSHEN

Nile River

Red Sea

1

2

3

N
E
S
W

For forty years, Moses and the Israelites wandered the desert on their way to the Promised Land.

CANAAN
THE PROMISED LAND

Jericho

Jerusalem

5

6

Kadesh-
Barnea

SINAI
NINSULA

Mount
Sinai

4

⇢ ROUTE

1. **MOSES IS BORN**
2. **PLAGUES**
3. **CROSSING THE RED SEA**
4. **THE TEN COMMANDMENTS**
5. **TIME-OUT**
6. **JOSHUA AND JERICHO**

HISTORICAL BOOKS

The Bible is a unique kind of **HISTORY**. It is the Story of God and His rescue plan to fix His broken relationship with people. It is **HIS STORY**. We can break up the Old Testament into four parts, based on the covenant God made with His people, and the land He promised Abraham:

1. **Before the Promised Land**—the Pentateuch
2. **In the Promised Land**—the time of the Judges and the Kings
3. **Kicked out of the Promised Land**—the exile
4. **Back to the Promised Land**—the Israelites return home

The part we call **HISTORICAL BOOKS** tells the story of Israel's time in the Promised Land. After the first five books of the Bible—called the Pentateuch—Joshua led God's people in battle, and they watched Him do amazing things. Then they finally came to live in the land God had promised to Abraham way back in Genesis.

As soon as they got there, the people started to break the covenant over and over again.

But God was patient. God was faithful. Even though they broke the covenant, He did not. God continued to love, provide for, and **RESCUE** His people.

HISTORICAL BOOKS

Joshua
Judges
Ruth
1 Samuel
2 Samuel
1 Kings
2 Kings
1 Chronicles
2 Chronicles
Ezra
Nehemiah
Esther

Just like the Pentateuch, the Historical Books point to Jesus as the **ONLY WAY** to fix our broken relationship with God. In the Historical Books, we see Jesus as the ultimate Conqueror, Judge, and King:

When Joshua met the mysterious commander of the army of the Lord . . . that was Jesus (Joshua 5:13–15).

When Judges shows us that God will keep sending His people a deliverer . . . that points to Jesus, our ultimate Deliverer (Judges 2:16; Romans 11:26–27).

When God promised David a Son who would become the forever King of Israel . . . He was talking about Jesus (2 Samuel 7:11–16).

JOSHUA
AND JERICHO

Remember the promises God made to Abraham?

"Your kids will become a great nation, they will have their own land, and from your family will come a blessing for the whole world!"

It had been nearly 500 years since God made those promises, and only the first one had come true. Sort of. Abraham's family **HAD** grown to be a nation—the Israelites. But they still didn't have their own land, and the "blessing for the whole world" was still unclear.

The Israelites had disobeyed God time and time again—so God put them in "time-out" until they were ready to obey Him.

Now, Israel's long time-out was finally over, and it was time to enter the **PROMISED LAND** once again.

Moses, their leader, gave a long speech, reminding the Israelite kids (who were now grown-ups) of everything God had done for them and all the laws He had given them. Everyone said, "Yes! We're going to trust God for **SURE** this time!"

And then Moses walked up on top of a mountain . . . and died.

Yep. He died. He got to see the Promised Land from the top of the mountain, but because he had disobeyed God, too, he never got to go in.

Instead, God chose **JOSHUA** to be Israel's new leader. Joshua was a man who trusted God.

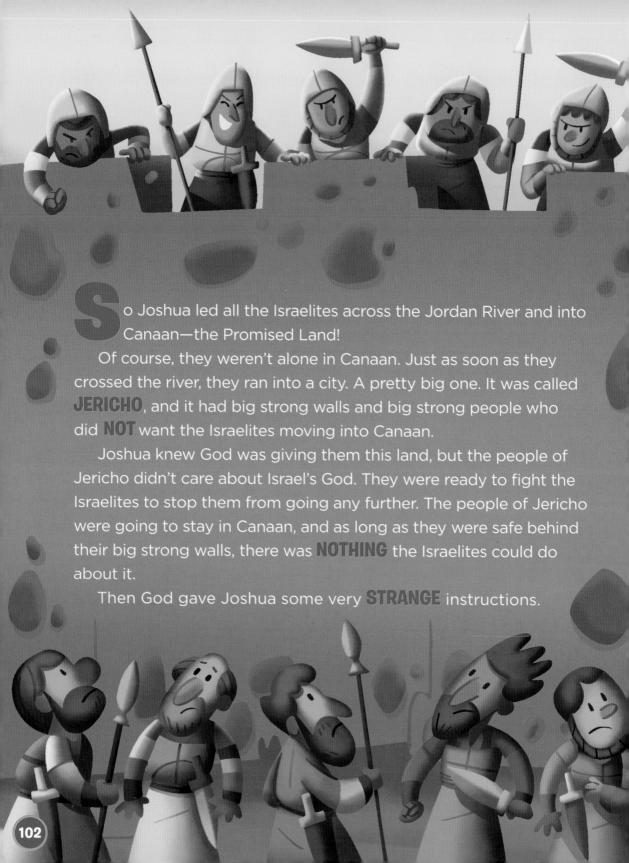

So Joshua led all the Israelites across the Jordan River and into Canaan—the Promised Land!

Of course, they weren't alone in Canaan. Just as soon as they crossed the river, they ran into a city. A pretty big one. It was called JERICHO, and it had big strong walls and big strong people who did NOT want the Israelites moving into Canaan.

Joshua knew God was giving them this land, but the people of Jericho didn't care about Israel's God. They were ready to fight the Israelites to stop them from going any further. The people of Jericho were going to stay in Canaan, and as long as they were safe behind their big strong walls, there was NOTHING the Israelites could do about it.

Then God gave Joshua some very STRANGE instructions.

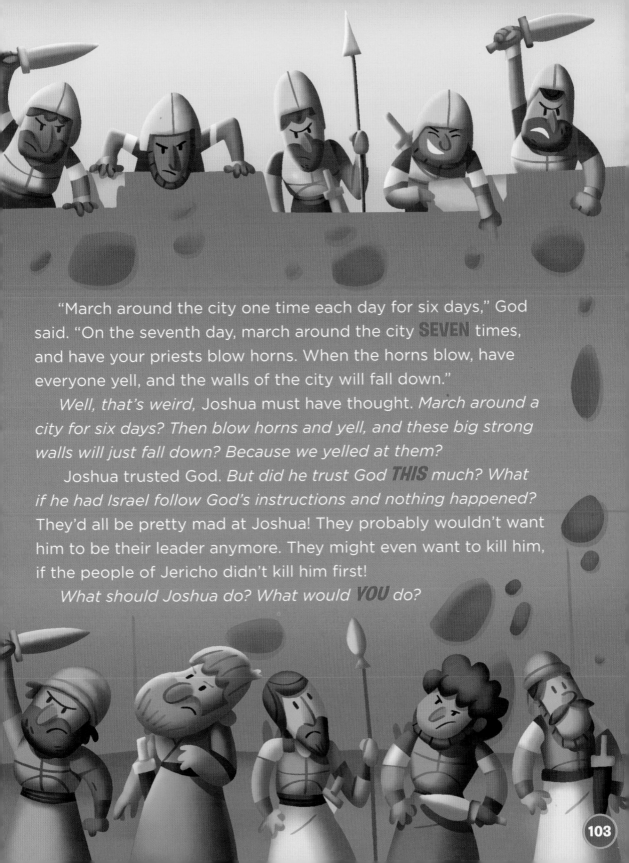

"March around the city one time each day for six days," God said. "On the seventh day, march around the city SEVEN times, and have your priests blow horns. When the horns blow, have everyone yell, and the walls of the city will fall down."

Well, that's weird, Joshua must have thought. *March around a city for six days? Then blow horns and yell, and these big strong walls will just fall down? Because we yelled at them?*

Joshua trusted God. *But did he trust God THIS much? What if he had Israel follow God's instructions and nothing happened?* They'd all be pretty mad at Joshua! They probably wouldn't want him to be their leader anymore. They might even want to kill him, if the people of Jericho didn't kill him first!

What should Joshua do? What would YOU do?

Joshua remembered how God had saved the Israelites— including him—from slavery in Egypt. He was there when God fed them in the desert. Plus, God had told Joshua that He had **ALREADY** given Jericho to him. *Doubt God?* Not Joshua! He had confidence in his **BIG STRONG GOD**.

Joshua led the Israelites as they marched around Jericho for six days. On the seventh day, he had them blow horns and yell, just like God said.

And the walls fell down.

The Israelites got to enter the Promised Land! And Joshua added **THIS** story to all the stories of an amazing God who could be trusted.

No matter what.

JOSHUA AND JERICHO
FAMILY CONNECTION

JOSHUA 1-6

EVERYDAY TRUTH

God gives me the strength to trust Him even when I don't understand what He is asking me to do!

TALK

Dear God . . .

Why do you think remembering God's faithfulness helped Joshua trust Him?

Share a time when you needed to trust God.

PRAY

Dear God, please give us strength like Joshua to trust You even when we don't understand what You are asking us to do. Amen.

Finally, Joshua and the Israelites

were living in Canaan, the land God had promised them!

It was **WONDERFUL** land! Canaan was filled with grapes and figs . . . fields for growing crops and raising animals . . . everything God's people needed. But it was also filled with Canaanites, Hittites, Amorites, Perizzites, Hivites, and Jebusites.

What are those? They sort of sound like bugs. Or diseases! But they were people. There were many different groups of people living in Canaan when the Israelites showed up.

This wasn't good, because God had told the Israelites that anyone else living in Canaan needed to **LEAVE**. You see, the other people in Canaan didn't follow Israel's God. They worshipped their own gods. The moon god. The sun god. The ocean god. The river god. Lots of made-up gods.

If Israel was going to be **HOLY**, set apart for God, then they couldn't bow down to any other gods. If they really believed their God was the true God, then they had to ignore all the gods that other people worshipped.

But they didn't.

Do you know what it's called when you ignore what you believe? When you walk away from your beliefs? It's called **APOSTASY**. *That's a fun word, isn't it?* And a *cycle* is "something that goes around and around." Like the wheels on a bicycle. Or a tricycle. Or a motorcycle.

At this point in history, Israel fell into a "cycle of apostasy," when they went **ROUND** and **ROUND**, believing, then not believing. Trusting God, then ignoring Him. It went something like this:

Because they didn't make all the other groups leave Canaan, the Israelites ended up living around people who worshipped other gods. Pretty soon, the Israelites started praying to those gods, too, breaking their promise to the one **TRUE** God!

God had warned Moses that if the Israelites worshipped other gods, He would no longer protect them from their **ENEMIES**. And that is exactly what happened. Israel bowed down to other gods, and God stopped protecting them. Then other nations came in and took over parts of Israel, making the Israelites slaves again.

Being a slave is a terrible thing, so the Israelites turned back to God and cried, "**HELP US**!" They said they were sorry for ignoring God. They promised never to ignore God again.

And so, God helped them. He would raise up a leader in Israel and help that leader **FREE** the people from their enemy. So the Israelites were happy. And they thanked God!

And then do you know what happened? The whole thing started all over! A cycle—round and round! Once the Israelites were safe and happy, they forgot about God **AGAIN**. They bowed down to other gods **AGAIN**.

It's like if you got in trouble for taking a cookie you weren't supposed to take. You got in **SO** much trouble that you said, "I'll never steal another cookie as long as I live!" And then, when you weren't in trouble anymore, you saw those cookies again and thought, *Those cookies look awfully good* . . . And so, you took a cookie . . . **AGAIN**!

This is what happened to Israel over and over for more than 250 years! When they were safe and happy, they would **FORGET** about God. So God would stop protecting them, and they'd get in big trouble. Then they'd be so unhappy they'd turn back to God and say, "**HELP US! WE WON'T DO IT AGAIN!**" So God would help them, and they'd be safe and happy again.

And then they'd see another cookie . . .

You get the idea. Bicycles are fun. Motorcycles are fun. *Aposta-cycles?* Not so much.

APOSTA-CYCLES
FAMILY CONNECTION

JOSHUA 24

EVERYDAY TRUTH

Because God never changes, I can trust Him faithfully.

TALK

What does *apostasy* mean?

Why do you think forgetting their beliefs made life hard for the Israelites?

Dear God . . .

PRAY

Dear God, thank You that even though our attitudes and actions change, You never change! Amen.

After the Israelites were living

in the Promised Land, Joshua died. Joshua had been a good leader. He trusted God.

But more than 250 years passed before Israel had a leader like Joshua again. Instead of having one leader who could help Israel follow God for a long time, Israel had a whole bunch of leaders who were raised up by God when there was trouble, and then disappeared when the trouble was over.

There are **TWELVE** of these leaders named in the Bible: Othniel, Ehud, Shamgar, Deborah, Gideon, Tola, Jair, Jephthah, Ibzan, Elon, Abdon, and Samson.

Do you notice that some of those names sound familiar, while others sound really crazy and weird? Have you ever met anyone named Othniel? Or Shamgar? How would YOU like to be named Othniel or Shamgar?

No? Well, who could blame you?

DEBORAH helped the Israelites when they were attacked by the Canaanites. **GIDEON** helped the Israelites when they were attacked by the Midianites. **JEPHTHAH** helped the Israelites when they were attacked by the Ammonites.

And then there was **SAMSON**. You've probably heard of him—he's like the Incredible Hulk of the Bible. God made Samson really, **REALLY** strong. So strong that he beat Israel's enemies, the Philistines, almost all by himself! He killed a lion and knocked down a temple with his bare hands!

But like many of the judges, Samson wasn't very strong at actually following God.

Samson wasn't just an **ORDINARY** Israelite. He was a Nazirite, which was a higher level of "set apart for God." Like, ninja-holy. To be a Nazirite, you couldn't ever drink wine. You couldn't ever touch a dead person or a dead animal. And—get this—you couldn't ever cut your hair. You just had to let it grow and grow and **GROW**.

Samson was really good at fighting the Philistines, but he was really bad at keeping his Nazirite promises. Once Samson killed a bunch of Philistines—not with his bare hands—but with a jawbone of a donkey. The donkey was dead, of course, which means Samson had touched something dead.

Oops.

He also ate honey from a beehive that he found inside the body of a dead lion, which is disgusting **AND** broke his promise not to touch dead things.

Double oops.

And then came his biggest broken promise of all. There was a Philistine woman named **DELILAH**, whom Samson thought was really cute. (Remember: the Philistines were his enemies!) She asked him if there was anything that would take his amazing strength away. And he said, "Sure . . . just cut my hair." *(Really, Samson?!)*

And so, she did. Samson's hair wasn't what made him **STRONG**. God made him strong. But Samson had promised he would never cut his hair. And there was Delilah, with a pair of scissors.

Triple oops!

God took Samson's strength away, because as good as he was at fighting the Philistines, he really **WASN'T** good at following God.

Just like Samson, all of Israel was messing up over and over, breaking their promises to God. And try as they might, not one of the twelve judges was able to help Israel for very long.

Clearly, if the Israelites were going to be God's holy people—and stay around long enough as a nation to bless the whole world—they were going to need a **STRONGER** leader, one who would listen to God—unlike Samson.

They would get one eventually, but it would take a very, very long time.

JUDGES
FAMILY CONNECTION

FUN FACTS

For 250 years Israel was without a true leader. *Can you imagine what it would be like to go to school in a classroom without a teacher?* It was like that . . . only worse! The word *judge* means "leader." Israel's judges were only temporary leaders that tried to help when things got tough. There were twelve judges, and none of them could keep Israel from disobeying God.

TALK

What made Samson and some of the other judges bad leaders?

Why do you think it's important to have good leaders to follow?

Dear God . . .

PRAY

Dear God, thank You for the good leaders in our lives. We pray for those who need Your help to lead well. Amen.

RUTH'S REDEEMER

In the days when Israel was ruled by judges, there lived a young woman named Ruth. Ruth wasn't an Israelite. She lived in a country called Moab, which was right next to Israel.

Ruth met a man from Israel, named Mahlon, and married him. Mahlon's brother was named Chilion. He met a girl in Moab whose name was Orpah. No, not Oprah—**ORPAH**. Chilion and Orpah got married too.

Mahlon and Chilion were living in Moab with their mom and dad because there was a **FAMINE** in Israel. (That means there wasn't enough food, just like when Joseph was in Egypt.) Their mom's name was Naomi, and their dad's name was Elimelech—which is fun to say over and over.

But one day (and this is terrible news), Elimelech died. Naomi no longer had a husband.

And then (this is even more terrible news), Mahlon and Chilion died—**BOTH** of them. Now Ruth and Orpah didn't have husbands, and Naomi, who'd already lost her husband, no longer had any sons.

Naomi was very sad. She decided she should go back to **ISRAEL**, since that's where she was from. She told Ruth and Orpah to stay in **MOAB**, since that's where they were from.

It would be good for Ruth and Orpah to stay in Moab, because they had friends and family there. They'd be okay.

But Naomi had no husband. She had no sons. Her home in Israel had been sold, so she had nowhere to live. And she was too old to work.

Orpah said goodbye to Naomi, and went back to her family. But Ruth didn't say goodbye. Instead, Ruth did something very **SURPRISING**.

"I will go to Israel with you," she said.

Even though Naomi wasn't part of Ruth's family. Even though Israel wasn't Ruth's country. Even though Israel's God wasn't the god of Moab. Ruth **LOVED** Naomi, and she wanted her to be okay. If Naomi had no home in Israel, Ruth would have no home with her!

"Your people will be my people, and your God will be my God," Ruth said.

How **AMAZING**! Ruth was willing to give up a lot to show love to Naomi!

God loves it when we show love. He loved it when Ruth showed love to Naomi. God wanted to help them, because that's what **HE** likes to do: help people.

Back in Israel, there was a man named **BOAZ** who loved God. Boaz also had a nice house and big fields. So he had plenty of food.

Boaz heard about the love Ruth had shown to Naomi. He heard how Ruth had left her own family and her own country so that Naomi wouldn't be alone.

God whispered in Boaz's heart that he should help Ruth and Naomi. So first, he let Ruth pick food from his fields—for **FREE**—so she and Naomi would have enough to eat.

Then—and this part is really amazing—he offered to make Ruth his **WIFE**, so she would have a home and a family again!

But what about Naomi? Boaz wanted to help her, too, so he redeemed the land that used to belong to Naomi and her husband, Elimelech, and gave it to Naomi as a present!

REDEEM means "to buy back." To pay a price so something—or someone—can be free. Now Naomi and Ruth were free from *poverty* (that means "being poor").

The story of Ruth and Naomi reminds us about God's **RESCUE** plan—His plan to set the whole world free from sin and death. Boaz had to pay a price to redeem Naomi's land, and just like Boaz, someone would need to pay a price to redeem the whole world.

RUTH'S REDEEMER
FAMILY CONNECTION

RUTH

TRICKY BITS

What does redeem mean?

To *redeem* means "to buy back, repurchase, or clear a debt." Just like Boaz redeemed Naomi's family land by buying it back and giving it to her as a gift, Jesus redeemed our lives by clearing our debt of sin and giving us the gift of eternal life.

TALK

Why do you think Ruth decided to stay with Naomi instead of returning to her home?

What are some ways we can love others the way Ruth faithfully loved Naomi?

Dear God . . .

PRAY

Dear God, thank You for all the ways You help us when we need You. Show us how to be faithful like Ruth and like You. Amen.

KING SAUL

The judges tried and tried to help

the Israelites live God's way. But the people just wouldn't listen. The Bible even says they "would not listen to their judges." The Israelites needed another leader.

SAMUEL was trying his best to help Israel follow God. *Who was Samuel?* He was a prophet of God. *What was a prophet?*

A **PROPHET** was "a person who delivered messages from God." God would speak to the prophet, and then the prophet would tell the people what God wanted them to do.

Since Israel didn't have a leader, prophets like Samuel would try to help them follow God. Whenever the Israelites wandered away from God, Samuel would say, "Hey! You're going the wrong way!" Samuel **TRIED** to get the Israelites to do the right things, but they didn't always listen—just like they hadn't listened to the judges. "You aren't our king!" they'd say, which was a little like saying, "You're not the boss of me!"

The Israelites kept messing up. They **IGNORED** God and His prophet. So God let Israel's enemies get the best of them. The Philistines attacked them over and over, taking their sheep and cows—even taking whole cities!

The Philistines were **BIG** and **STRONG**. They knew how to make swords and spears out of iron. These were harder and stronger than the bronze swords and spears of the Israelites. The Israelites were scared of the Philistines!

"We need a king to protect us!" the Israelites told Samuel.

"But God is your king!" Samuel said.

The Israelites didn't want **GOD** to be their king. They wanted a human to be their king, just like the nations around them. Someone big and **TALL** and strong. Someone who could wear fancy robes and ride out in front of them on a fancy horse. Someone who looked **IMPRESSIVE**!

Finally, God said, "Fine. You want a king? You can have a king."

Samuel asked God who should be Israel's first king and God said, "**SAUL**."

Saul looked like a king. He was tall. He was strong. He was handsome. He was exactly what Israel wanted.

"**HOORAY**!" they shouted. "Now we'll be safe!"

And they were safe . . . for a while. Saul's first battle against the Philistines was a **BIG** success. The Israelites won!

"Hooray for King Saul!" they shouted.

Tall, strong, and brave, Saul was good at fighting battles. But he wasn't very good at following God's **DIRECTIONS**. Samuel would tell Saul what God wanted him to do, and sometimes Saul would do the exact opposite! If Samuel said, "God wants you to go right," Saul would go left! If Samuel said, "God wants you to go up," Saul would go down!

How could the Israelites be God's people if their leader wouldn't do what God said?

Israel needed a leader who would help them be a **HOLY** nation. They needed a leader who would help them follow God's rules, so they could live with Him and bring the **BLESSING** that would save the whole world *(remember God's promise to Abraham?)* The blessing that would rescue God's creation from sin!

Having a godly leader for Israel was really, **REALLY** important. Even though Saul **LOOKED** like a good king, he wasn't a good king because he didn't listen to God. In his heart, he didn't really want to do what God said.

Israel needed a new king. A **GODLY** king. A king who wanted to follow God with his whole heart.

God told Samuel He was going to pick a new king for Israel, and the person He was going to pick would surprise them all!

KING SAUL
FAMILY CONNECTION

1 SAMUEL 8-10

EVERYDAY TRUTH

Because God is the King of my life, I must obey and honor Him!

TALK

Why did Israel want Saul to be their king?

Why do you think it's important for us to obey and follow God?

Dear God . . .

PRAY

Dear God, thank You for being the King of our hearts. Please lead us the right way so our lives will bring honor to You. Amen.

DAVID AND GOLIATH

This must be the guy! Israel's new king!" Samuel said.

Samuel was looking at Eliab, the oldest son of a man named Jesse. God had sent Samuel to Jesse's house to find the new king for Israel.

Eliab, Jesse's oldest son, looked like he'd make a **GREAT** king! He was tall and strong and good-looking. Just like Saul!

But God said, "No. Not him."

Was Samuel confused? Maybe. Eliab **REALLY** did look impressive. But God told Samuel, "You're looking at the outside of this man. I look on the inside."

So Jesse brought out his next son. "This one?" Samuel asked God.

"No," God replied. "Not him either."

Samuel tried the next son, and the one after that, and the one after that. **SEVEN** sons in all!

And each time God said, "No."

There were no more sons to meet—or so Samuel thought. Samuel asked Jesse, "Is that all?"

"There is one more," Jesse said. "The youngest. He's outside, taking care of the sheep."

Jesse called in his youngest son, **DAVID**. David didn't look like a king—he looked like a kid.

But God said, "That's the one."

Samuel poured olive oil on David's head as a sign that he was being **SET APART** for God in a very special way. Someday, David would be Israel's king. He would follow God with his **WHOLE** heart. And through David, Jesse's youngest son, would come the long-awaited blessing for the whole world.

For now, King Saul needed David's big brothers to fight the Philistines. David's brothers were all big and strong enough to join Saul's army. But not David. Instead of fighting, David brought food to his brothers. And one day, while he was visiting them in Saul's army, David saw **GOLIATH**.

Goliath was a giant, Philistine warrior. The biggest, tallest, strongest man they had ever seen!

The Philistines challenged King Saul. "If **YOUR** strongest man can beat **OUR** strongest man, we will be your slaves. But if our strongest man can beat your strongest man, you will be our slaves!"

SOMEONE had to fight Goliath. *But who was brave enough? Who was big enough? Who was strong enough?*

"I'll do it!" a voice called out.

King Saul turned around and couldn't believe his eyes. It was **DAVID**, Jesse's youngest son—and just a kid, at that!

Naw, the king must have thought. *I don't think so.*

"You're too young," he told David.

"God has helped me save our sheep from a lion and a bear," David said, "and God will help me save Israel from Goliath!"

It sounded **CRAZY**, but King Saul didn't know what else to do. No one else was brave enough to fight Goliath!

"Here. Use my sword," King Saul said.

"No, thank you," David answered. "It's too big for me."

Instead of a sword, David took the **SLINGSHOT** he used to protect his sheep from other animals. Then he picked up five smooth stones and walked onto the battlefield to meet Goliath.

ook at you! You're like a little stick," Goliath laughed, "and I'll break you into pieces and feed you to the birds!"

But David wasn't scared, because David trusted God.

"This battle belongs to **GOD**, and He is going to help me strike you down!" David yelled.

Then David put a stone in his sling and swung it around and around his head. He let go and the stone flew through the air— and hit Goliath right between the eyes!

The great, strong giant wobbled, then fell down dead!

Israel was **SAVED**!

WHO *had defeated Goliath?* Not big, strong King Saul. Not Jesse's warrior sons.

It was little **DAVID**. The one who was supposed to be taking care of the sheep.

David trusted God. And when we trust God with everything, God can use us to do amazing things.

Even if we're small!

DAVID AND GOLIATH
FAMILY CONNECTION

1 SAMUEL 16-17

FUN FACTS

The Philistine giant, Goliath, stood tall—roughly nine feet tall. In addition to his large stature, Goliath wore armor that weighed 5,000 shekels—that's 125 pounds! David, on the other hand, went into battle with no armor because it was too heavy for him to wear. With only five stones, a sling, and great faith in God, young David defeated Israel's largest enemy.

TALK

Why did God choose David to be king even though he was young?

What "giants" are you facing right now?

Dear God . . .

PRAY

Dear God, thank You for giving us the strength to win the battles we face every day. Help us to find courage in who You say we are. Amen.

ISRAEL'S NEW KING

As you can imagine, defeating the giant Goliath and saving Israel made David pretty popular. Everyone in Israel wanted to be David's friend—even King Saul!

When David was old enough, the king asked him to be a **LEADER** in the army. David might not have been the tallest or strongest, but even King Saul could see that David followed God.

Every time David went out to fight a battle, God was with him and David **WON**. So King Saul sent David to fight more battles. And David kept on winning!

At first this made King Saul very happy. But as David kept winning, the king became less happy.

You see, the more David won, the more **POPULAR** David became.

"Hooray for David!" the people would yell every time they saw him.

King Saul got **JEALOUS**.

Do you know what jealous means? To be *jealous* is "to want something that someone else has." With all this winning, David was now more popular than King Saul. If David kept winning, eventually the people would want **HIM** to be king!

King Saul was jealous of David's popularity. He was jealous of all of David's victories. He was jealous that God was with David.

So King Saul got **ANGRY**.

Have you ever been so angry that you did something that wasn't very smart? Like throw your favorite toy against the wall or yell at your best friend?

Yep. Anger can make us do bad things.

As King Saul's anger grew, he decided he wanted to do a really bad thing. He wanted to kill David.

That's right. Even though David was helping King Saul win all these battles. Even though David was helping keep Israel **SAFE**.

David knew that King Saul wanted to kill him. It's a bad thing when a king wants to kill you, because the whole army obeys the king, whether they want to or not. Now the whole army would try to kill David too!

BUT David had a best friend who wanted to help. His best friend's name was **JONATHAN**. Jonathan promised he would tell David if King Saul was planning to hurt him. *How would Jonathan know?* Because Jonathan was King Saul's son!

Jonathan didn't want his father, the king, to kill his friend David. So when Jonathan heard his father making a plan to kill David, he ran to David and told him.

David knew he couldn't stay around King Saul or his best friend, Jonathan, anymore. So David ran away from King Saul and his army. He hid in the desert. He hid in caves. He waited for God to tell him what to do next.

How long do you think David ran from King Saul? A week? A month?

EIGHT YEARS.

That's right. David ran and hid from King Saul and his whole army for eight years! But God was with David, and God kept David safe.

Then one day, there was a great **BATTLE** between the Philistines and King Saul's army. Many Israelites died in the battle. David's best friend, Jonathan, was one of them. So was Jonathan's father, King Saul. Both of them died in the battle.

David was very sad to hear that so many Israelites had been killed. He was especially sad to hear that his friend Jonathan had died. He was even sad to hear that King Saul had died.

Now Israel needed a new king. *Who should they choose? Who would help them be victorious in battle? Who would help them* **FOLLOW GOD**?

The Israelites thought about it. And they remembered who had been following God all along. They remembered who God had helped win all those battles before he'd been forced to run for his life. David!

In time, Jesse's youngest son, **DAVID**, would become Israel's king. And what a king he would be!

ISRAEL'S NEW KING
FAMILY CONNECTION

2 SAMUEL 2

EVERYDAY TRUTH

I don't need to compare myself to others because God made me the right way!

TALK

Why was Saul jealous of David?

Share a time you struggled with jealousy.

Dear God . . .

PRAY

Dear God, it is never helpful to compare ourselves to others. Please show us the unique way You made us according to Your plan. Amen.

GOD'S PROMISE TO DAVID

When David was 30 years old, he became king of Israel. David was a good king.

He followed God. He listened to God. He talked to God. He even wrote songs about God! We call them psalms, which is a Greek word that means "songs."

God helped David. First, He helped David defeat the Philistines to keep Israel safe. Then, God helped David capture JERUSALEM, a big city that was right in the middle of the land God had promised them.

With God's help, David made Jerusalem the new capital of Israel and the place the Israelites would worship God.

David promised he would always follow God. And in return, God made a PROMISE to David.

Do you remember the promises God made to Abraham? Abraham's kids would become a great nation, they would have their own land, and from Abraham's family—the Israelites—would come a blessing for the whole world.

With David as king, Israel really DID become a great nation. They were safe in the land God had promised. They didn't know exactly how Israel would bless the "whole world," but they had some clues. Then God gave David his own SPECIAL promise. God promised David that someone from his family would rule over God's people. Not for a year . . . or ten years . . . or even 100 years.

Forever.

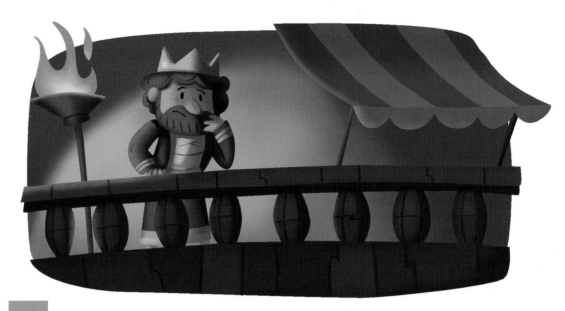

That sounds a little crazy, doesn't it? How could one family stay on the throne **FOREVER**? Even David wasn't sure how that would work!

And did it have anything to do with the blessing for the whole world? A forever kind of blessing might need a forever kind of king, right?

God's rescue plan was getting interesting!

David was a good king, but he wasn't perfect. David sinned too. In fact, David did something **REALLY** terrible.

When King David was older, he was looking out from the roof of his palace one day when he saw a woman. The woman's name was **BATHSHEBA**, and she was so pretty that King David decided he wanted her to be his wife.

That's not a terrible thing, right? Not all by itself. What made it terrible was that Bathsheba was **ALREADY** married. She was someone else's wife! Besides, David was **ALREADY** married. He even had kids.

But King David was feeling selfish. He thought to himself, *I'm the king, and the king should get whatever he wants.*

David wanted Bathsheba to be his wife, even though she was someone else's wife. *But what would he do about Bathsheba's husband?*

Have you ever done something bad and then because of that bad thing ended up doing something even **WORSE**?

That's what King David did. He wanted to be married to Bathsheba—so he had Bathsheba's husband **KILLED**.

You probably just spit out your milk and yelled, "He did **WHAT**?" It was a terrible thing. King David hoped nobody would ever find out what he had done.

But God knew. God sent a **PROPHET** named Nathan to tell David He knew about his big sin. David didn't make excuses. He didn't say, "But I'm the king!" David fell down on the ground and said he was sorry. He asked God to forgive him—to make his heart clean again.

God **FORGAVE** David. But King David's sin hurt his whole family. The son he had with Bathsheba got sick and died. Another one of David's son's became so angry that he tried to kill David so he could become king himself!

When King David didn't follow God, it hurt a lot of people. But God still kept His promise to David. Another one of David's sons became king after David died, and David's grandson after that, and on and on.

Even though David messed up, God kept His **PROMISE**.

We all mess up—in little ways, and in big ways. But when we make a mistake, God never gives up on us. God loves us **ALWAYS**. Even when we mess up!

GOD'S PROMISE TO DAVID
FAMILY CONNECTION

2 SAMUEL 7

TRICKY BITS

If we love and follow God, why do we still make mistakes?

Because of God's big love, He created us with free will, which means we are free to make our own choices. Without free will, we would be controlled by God to do whatever He wanted us to do. But that's not the kind of relationship God wanted with His children. We all mess up sometimes. Because of Jesus, we can be forgiven and learn through our mistakes how to live God's way.

TALK

Dear God . . .

Why did God keep His promise even though David messed up?

What should you remember the next time you make a mistake?

PRAY

Dear God, thank You for never giving up on us! When we mess up, we trust You to help us make things right with others and with You. Amen.

Imagine if someone came up to you

and said, "Ask me for anything you want, and I will give it to you."

What would you ask for?

All the **TOYS** *in the world?*

All the **PIZZA** *in the world?*

The talent to be a basketball star? Soccer star? Movie star?

Most people would probably ask for money, or fame, or power. But **SOLOMON** wasn't like most people.

Solomon was David's son. Not the son who tried to kill David—no, that was Absalom. Absalom didn't get to be king.

Instead, Absalom's brother Solomon became Israel's next king. And not long after Solomon became king, he had a **DREAM**. A very interesting dream.

You see, God showed up in Solomon's dream.

What did God look like? We don't know. *How did Solomon know it was God?* We don't know. Maybe when you see God, you just know it's God!

Anyway, God showed up in Solomon's dream. And God said, "Ask me for anything, Solomon, and I will give it to you."

Whoa.

Anything!

What would **YOU** *ask for?*

Solomon's dad, David, was a **GREAT** king. Solomon probably wanted to be a great king too.

If Solomon was really, really rich—if he had more gold and silver than anyone in the world—everyone would think he was a great king. In the ancient world, great kings usually had lots and lots of gold and silver. Great riches impressed **EVERYONE**!

But that isn't what Solomon asked for.

If Solomon was really, really famous—if all the other kings wanted to visit him and wanted to be friends with him and give him gifts—everyone would think he was a great king. Great fame impressed everyone!

But that isn't what Solomon asked for.

Nope. Instead, Solomon asked for **WISDOM**.

Wisdom is "the ability to make good choices."

Solomon asked to be wise when he could have asked for **ANYTHING**!

Why did Solomon ask for wisdom instead of money or fame— or pizza?

Because Solomon knew something. He knew that being a good king was all about making **GOOD** choices. Like when to go to war, when **NOT** to go to war, how to solve problems in your kingdom, how to bring peace when people are angry, or how to lead. Wisdom would help Solomon do all of these things.

It turns out that asking for wisdom was a very **WISE** choice.

God told Solomon that since he'd asked for wisdom instead of riches and fame, not only would God make Solomon wise, but He would also make him rich and famous!

And that's **EXACTLY** what God did. Solomon became very wise. He could solve all sorts of problems. No matter what happened, it seemed like Solomon **ALWAYS** knew the right thing to do.

And Solomon's good choices made Israel very rich! Solomon had gold and silver and horses—more than any other king Israel would ever have!

Kings and queens from other countries heard about Solomon's wisdom and riches and traveled to Israel to visit him. They wanted to be Solomon's friends and ask him for **ADVICE**. They brought him expensive gifts, which made Solomon and Israel even richer!

All of this happened because God showed up in Solomon's dream, and Solomon decided that wisdom—or the ability to make good decisions—was the most valuable gift of all!

If God could give you just one thing, what would you ask for?

SOLOMON'S WISDOM
FAMILY CONNECTION

1 KINGS 3

EVERYDAY TRUTH

Wisdom helps me make the right choice.

TALK

What does it mean to be *wise?*

What are some ways we can use wisdom in our lives?

Dear God . . .

PRAY

Dear God, we know that wisdom comes from You. May we always look to You in prayer and Bible reading to figure out what to do. Amen.

BAD KINGS

Israel had asked God for a king.
Even though God was their true King and leader, Israel decided they wanted a human king, just like the other nations.

God gave them Saul to be their king. Saul started out okay, but didn't stay that way for very long. **SAUL** wasn't a good king.

Then came David. **DAVID** was a good king. Yes, there was that time he killed a man so he could take his wife. That was bad. But he was very, very sorry and asked God to forgive him. He wasn't perfect, but overall, David was a good king.

Then came **SOLOMON**, David's son. Like Saul, Solomon started out okay. But he didn't stay that way either. He forced the Israelites to build him big, fancy palaces. And Solomon married women from other countries who worshipped other gods. Pretty soon Solomon was worshipping other gods too!

And then things really went downhill. Solomon's son **REHOBOAM** became king. He was so mean to the Israelites that half of them said, "We don't want you to be our king!" They picked a guy named **JEROBOAM** to be their king instead.

Now Israel had **TWO** kings!

No country can have two kings at the same time, so can you guess what happened?

Israel split in two. The northern half of Israel followed Jeroboam, and the southern half followed Rehoboam. Israel, God's chosen nation, was no longer one nation. It was two nations, and neither of them was doing a very good job of following God.

In the north, Nadab became king afterJeroboam, and he was just as bad. Then Baasha became king. Just as bad. Then Elah, then Zimri. **BAD** and **DOUBLE BAD**!

You'd think everyone would learn a lesson from all these bad kings. But they didn't. The next king of the north was Omri, and the Bible says he "did more evil than **ALL** the kings before him!"

Omri's son Ahab was even worse. Not only did Ahab not follow God, but he and his wife, Jezebel, tried to kill everyone who **DID** follow God!

Things weren't much better down south.
After Rehoboam and Jeroboam split Israel in half, the two halves of Israel had **39 KINGS** over the next **400 YEARS**—thirty-nine kings! And almost all of them were bad!

All these bad kings were a problem for a couple of reasons. First, bad kings make bad decisions, and bad decisions aren't good for **ANYBODY**.

Second, way back in the time of Moses, God promised he would protect Israel from their enemies as long as they followed God. If Israel **STOPPED** following God, God would stop protecting Israel.

Remember the time of the judges? The Israelites would turn away from God, and then—**BOOM**!—one of their enemies would attack them and take over a few cities.

Well . . . 400 years later, Israel's enemies were **HUGE**. Israel's new enemies were so big they weren't just kingdoms anymore—they were **EMPIRES**, and that changed everything!

BAD KINGS
FAMILY CONNECTION

1 KINGS 12-16

FUN FACTS

During the reign of Solomon's son Rehoboam, around 930 BC, Israel split into two kingdoms— the kingdom of Israel in the north, including the tribes of Asher, Dan, Ephraim, Gad, Issachar, Manasseh, Naphtali, Reuben, Simeon, and Zebulun, and the kingdom of Judah in the south, made up of the tribes of Judah and Benjamin.

TALK

Why did Israel split in two?

What was so bad about Israel's bad kings?

Dear God . . .

PRAY

Dear God, even when our leaders make bad choices, help us choose to live Your way. Amen.

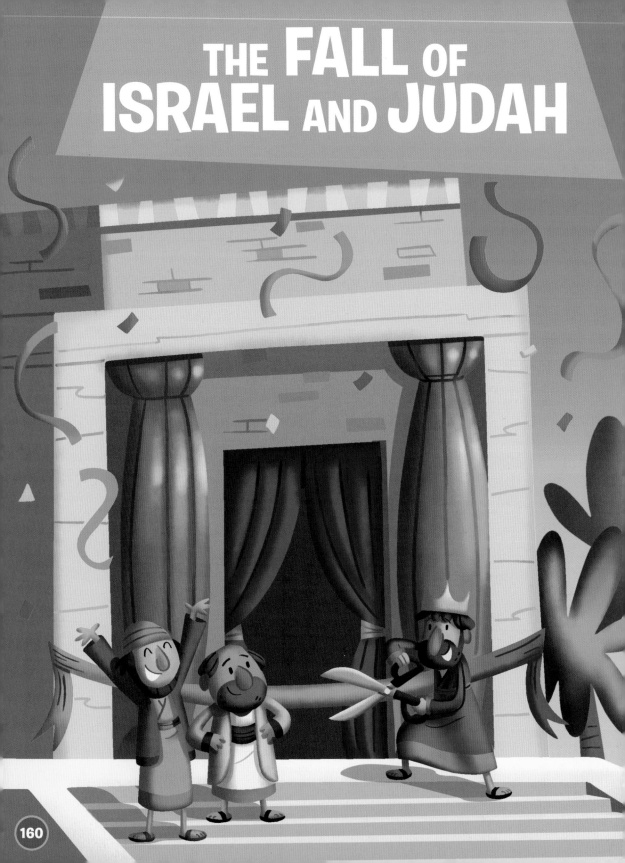

THE FALL OF ISRAEL AND JUDAH

Though he wasn't a perfect king,

Solomon did do some good things when he was king. One of the best things he did was build a new temple for God. It was a **BEAUTIFUL** temple that took seven years to build!

When Solomon's new temple was finished, all the Israelites came together to **CELEBRATE**. Solomon gave a long speech and reminded them of something very important. Solomon said that as long as the Israelites **FOLLOWED** God, He would bless them and protect them. If they **IGNORED** God, or started following other gods, then enemies would come and carry them out of the Promised Land.

Solomon wasn't the first one to say this. Moses had said the same thing, way back at Mount Sinai. This warning had been repeated over and **OVER**.

Follow God, and things will be wonderful. Turn away from God, and enemies will carry you out of this special land.

The Israelites were no longer following God. King after king worshipped other gods—and even killed the Israelites who wanted to follow the one true God!

Yet God was patient. He sent prophets to warn the Israelites again and again.

"Turn back to God!" they'd say. "Or there will be trouble!"

But Israel's kings **IGNORED** the prophets. They **IGNORED** the warnings. They forgot about God.

And eventually, God couldn't wait any longer. He had to do what He had promised He would do, even though it made Him very sad.

Two great empires were growing next to Israel. In the north were the **ASSYRIANS**. In the south, the **BABYLONIANS**. Their kings were the strongest kings with the biggest armies the world had ever seen, and they were always at war, conquering one nation after another. It seemed like they were taking over the whole world!

Finally, God stopped protecting the northern kingdom of Israel. The Assyrian army attacked Israel and **DESTROYED** it. The king and many of the Israelites were dragged away to Assyria in chains.

The northern kingdom no longer existed.

God was even more patient with the southern kingdom, called Judah, since the kings of Judah were the children of King David. But for every good king of Judah, there were two bad kings. For every king who turned back to God, there were **TWO** more who wandered even farther away.

About 100 years after the Assyrians attacked the northern kingdom, God removed His protection from Judah in the south. Many of the people of Judah were dragged away to Babylon, which was ruled by an evil king named NEBUCHADNEZZAR.

Next, King Nebuchadnezzar and the Babylonians captured David's city, Jerusalem. What's worse, Jerusalem was BURNED! The walls were pulled down, and Solomon's temple—God's dwelling place among the Israelites—was completely destroyed.

Was this the end of God's people? Was it the end of God's rescue plan? Would the blessing for the whole world ever come?

THE FALL OF ISRAEL AND JUDAH
FAMILY CONNECTION

2 KINGS 25

FUN FACTS

It took King Solomon seven years to build God's temple, which had two sections separated by a veil—the Holy Place and the Most Holy Place. The temple was 60 cubits (90 feet) long, 20 cubits (30 feet) wide, and 30 cubits (45 feet) high. Almost 400 years after it was built, the temple was destroyed by the Babylonians in 587–586 BC.

TALK

What are some ways God showed His patience with Israel?

Why did God stop protecting the kingdoms of Israel?

Dear God . . .

PRAY

Dear God, thank You for being patient with us as we learn what it means to honor You. Amen.

Do you know what an empire is?

An *empire* is "a bunch of countries and a bunch of people all ruled by just one king." A **MEGA-KING**. There were a lot of mega-kings in the Bible. These mega-kings had mega-armies, too. If an empire wanted your land, they would probably just take it.

Some of these mega-kings got so big they started to think of themselves as gods. They even made their people bow down and worship them, as if they were gods! But they weren't gods. God was still God—the **ONLY** God. And God used mega-kings and their mega-armies to do His *will*—that means "to get what He wanted done."

First, God let the Assyrian army take over the northern kingdom of **ISRAEL**. Then He let the Babylonian army take over the southern kingdom of **JUDAH**.

Why?

Because God keeps His promises. He had promised the Israelites they would be safe as long as they followed Him. He also promised if they didn't follow Him, their enemies would carry them away.

It was a sad time for the Israelites. But God still loved them. He wanted them to have **HOPE**. Through two of His prophets, Isaiah and Jeremiah, God told the Israelites, long before it happened, that they would have to live in Babylon for seventy years. Then a new king would appear who would let them go back home.

God even told them the new king's name: **CYRUS**.

And sure enough, seventy years after the Israelites were carried off to Babylon, a new empire arose in the world. The Persian Empire. It was the **BIGGEST** empire anyone had ever seen, so big that it took over the Assyrian and Babylonian empires at the same time!

This new empire had a new king. *Can you guess his name?*

Yep. Cyrus.

And just as Jeremiah and Isaiah had foretold—more than a century before Cyrus was even born—Cyrus told the Israelites they could go back home. Back to Jerusalem and the Promised Land!

So, 50,000 Israelites packed up all their things and walked all the way back to Jerusalem. They rebuilt their houses. They rebuilt God's temple.

A priest named **EZRA**, who loved God very much, moved back to Jerusalem to teach the Israelites how to follow God again. Ezra read God's laws to them, and they promised to follow the one true God, no matter what!

Another Israelite, named **NEHEMIAH**, was still in Babylon, working for the king. King Cyrus had died, and the new king was Artaxerxes, which is a very fun name to say. It has two *x*'s. *Don't you wish your name had two X's?*

A visitor from Jerusalem told Nehemiah that the temple was rebuilt, but the walls of Jerusalem were still broken down. Walls were important in the ancient world, because walls protected people from their enemies. Until Jerusalem's walls were fixed, the city would **NEVER** be safe!

Nehemiah went to King Artaxerxes and asked if he could go back to Jerusalem to rebuild the walls. He even asked if the king would give him the supplies he needed to do the big job. *And guess what?* King Artaxerxes said **YES**! He gave Nehemiah what he needed to rebuild the walls and make Jerusalem safe again.

God used King Cyrus, King Artaxerxes, and the giant Persian Empire to help His people, the Israelites. These powerful kings, who thought **THEY** were gods, ended up helping the people of the real God move back home and rebuild their city!

Isn't it amazing how God can use anything or anyone—even kings who don't follow Him—to get what He wants done?

GOD GETS IT DONE
FAMILY CONNECTION

NEHEMIAH 1-2

EVERYDAY TRUTH

God can use anything or anyone to get what He wants done!

TALK

Why do you think God can use anything or anyone to get what He wants done?

What is something God can use you to get done?

Dear God . . .

PRAY

Dear God, thank You for inviting us to be a part of the good work You are doing. Show us how we can help to get what You want done. Amen.

BRAVE QUEEN ESTHER

A long time after King Cyrus had died, his grandson Xerxes became king. Xerxes was also called Ahasuerus, which sounds like a name for a dinosaur. So we'll just call him **XERXES**.

Xerxes was not as good a king as Cyrus. He wasn't as smart or as wise as Cyrus. And he had a bad temper.

Xerxes had a wife named **VASHTI**, who was very beautiful. Xerxes wanted to show his beautiful wife off to his friends at a party one night, but Vashti wouldn't come out of her room.

"Come out!" Xerxes said.

"No!" Vashti told him.

This made Xerxes angry. So angry that he threw Queen Vashti out of his palace and said she wasn't his queen anymore. Yep, Xerxes had a bad temper, all right!

Xerxes' friends said, "You need a **NEW** queen. An even better queen!"

Xerxes searched throughout the Persian Empire for the best queen of all.

And Xerxes found **ESTHER**.

Esther was an orphan—she had no mother or father. Esther lived with her cousin **MORDECAI**, who worked for King Xerxes at his palace.

But more important, Esther was a **JEW**.

What's a Jew? God's people were called the "Israelites," because they were the children of Israel. After Israel split in two, the southern half was called "Judah." People from Judah who ended up living in the Persian Empire were called "Jews."

King Xerxes didn't know Esther was a Jew. He just knew she was very pretty and very kind. The king liked Esther so much, he made her the new **QUEEN**!

Then things got complicated.

King Xerxes had a friend named **HAMAN**. And Haman didn't like Jews at all. Haman especially didn't like Esther's cousin Mordecai because Mordecai wouldn't bow down to Haman.

Have you ever met someone who wanted to be the boss of everyone? Haman was that kind of person.

Like Xerxes, Haman had a bad temper. Over and over he **DEMANDED** that Mordecai bow to him, and over and over Mordecai refused. Finally, Haman was so angry he wanted to kill Mordecai.

Then Haman had an even worse idea. *Why kill only Mordecai? Why not kill all the Jews in Persia?*

Haman lied and told King Xerxes that the Jews were troublemakers and that the Persian Empire would be better if there were no Jews. King Xerxes trusted Haman.

So the king signed a paper announcing that all the Jews would be **KILLED**. He hung the paper outside his palace, where Mordecai worked. Mordecai couldn't believe his eyes.

"Esther!" Mordecai said. "You have to go talk to the king!"

Esther was **TERRIFIED**. No one talked to the king without being invited. If you walked into the king's room without an invitation, you could be killed. **EVEN** if you were the queen!

But Mordecai said, "Esther, you can save your people. Maybe this is why you became queen!"

So Esther gathered her **COURAGE** and walked into the king's room. She waited to see if the guards would grab her and kill her! But King Xerxes said, "Let her talk to me."

Esther invited the king to a banquet and at that banquet, she invited him to another one. By the second meal, Esther had gathered enough courage to tell the king about Haman's plan.

"Someone is going to **KILL** my whole family and me!" she said.

King Xerxes was angry. *Who would try to kill his queen?*

Esther pointed to Haman.

"Haman," she said. "Haman plans to kill all the Jews. And I am a Jew!"

King Xerxes was **FURIOUS**. "Whatever you were going to do to the Jews," he said to Haman, "will be done to you!"

And that was the last time anyone had to worry about Haman.

God used the bravery of Esther, an orphan girl who became a queen, to **SAVE** the children of Israel.

BRAVE QUEEN ESTHER
FAMILY CONNECTION

ESTHER

EVERYDAY TRUTH

When I follow God, He leads me to do great things— right here, right now.

TALK

Why do you think God allowed Esther to become queen during this time?

What is the best thing about being where you are right now?

Dear God . . .

PRAY

Dear God, we are honored to be a part of Your plan—right now, right where we are. Show us ways we can serve You and serve others. Amen.

WOMEN OF THE BIBLE

The Bible is full of stories about amazing women who played an important role in God's rescue plan. You can read about many of them in this Bible, then explore the stories and strengths of other women on your own. As you learn about each woman of the Bible, talk about how their **GIRL POWER** inspires **YOU**!

TURN TO THE FOLLOWING PAGES TO READ THE FULL BIBLE STORIES OF THESE IMPORTANT WOMEN:

"BLESSED IS SHE WHO HAS BELIEVED THAT THE LORD WOULD FULFILL HIS PROMISES TO HER." Luke 1:45 (NIV)

REBEKAH

Her Story: Genesis 24
Her Strength: Service

DEBORAH

Her Story: Judges 4–5
Her Strength: Wisdom

HANNAH

Her Story: 1 Samuel 1
Her Strength: Prayer

ELIZABETH

Her Story: Luke 1
Her Strength: Honor

MARY *(Martha's Sister)*

Her Story: Luke 10:38–42
Her Strength: Focus

LYDIA

Her Story: Acts 16:11–15
Her Strength: Generosity

WRITINGS AND PROPHETS

The **WRITINGS** and **PROPHETS** tell the story of the last two sections of the Old Testament:

1. **Before the Promised Land**—the Pentateuch
2. **In the Promised Land**—the Historical Books
3. **Kicked out of the Promised Land**—the exile
4. **Back to the Promised Land**—the Israelites return home

In the Historical Books, God was faithful even when His people were not. God had made a *covenant* or "agreement" that said if the people turned away from God, He would kick them out of the Promised Land. God's people broke the covenant for 490 years before He finally decided He had to do something.

God didn't want to punish His people. But it was the only way to bring them back to Him.

The prophets said if the people would repent and turn back to God, He would bring them home and give them a whole new covenant. A covenant they could keep, because God Himself would live in their hearts and change them from the inside out.

WRITINGS AND PROPHETS

Job

Psalms

Proverbs

Ecclesiastes

Song of Solomon

Isaiah

Jeremiah

Lamentations

Ezekiel

Daniel

Hosea

Joel

Amos

Obadiah

Jonah

Micah

Nahum

Habakkuk

Zephaniah

Haggai

Zechariah

Malachi

Just like the Pentateuch and the Historical Books, the Writings and Prophets point to Jesus as the **ONLY WAY** to fix our broken relationship with God. In the Writings and Prophets:

When the Psalms spoke of a Messiah who would die for our sins . . . that was Jesus (Psalm 2:6–7; 22:1; 89:27).

When Isaiah declared that a new king would arise from the family of David . . . that was Jesus (Isaiah 11).

When Isaiah prophesied about a Messiah who would live as a servant and suffer and die for the sins of the people . . . that was Jesus (Isaiah 53).

HE GIVES AND TAKES AWAY

Once, a long, long time ago, there was a man named Job.

Job was a **RIGHTEOUS** man (that means he was a good guy). Just like Noah, he tried to do what was right. He listened to God. And God blessed Job. Job had ten kids, 7,000 sheep, 3,000 camels, 500 pair of oxen . . . **EVERYTHING** he ever wanted! Job had a really good life.

"Look at Job," God said. "He loves Me, and he does what's right!"

But then God's enemy, the sneaky ol' snake that had lied to Adam and Eve, said, "He only loves You because you've blessed him! Take away all his stuff, and he'll stop loving You for sure!"

"Let's see if you're right," God said.

Then that sneaky ol' snake—his real name is Satan—disappeared and—**BOOM**! Satan sent bandits, who stole Job's oxen and donkeys. Then he caused a fire that burned up all of Job's sheep. Then more bandits came and took his camels. Then, worst of all, a windstorm knocked down the house where Job's kids were, and they all died!

Job was **VERY** sad! He ripped his clothes—that's what people used to do long ago when they were sad—and he sat in the dirt. *But did he stop loving God?*

Nope. Job said, "God gave me all these things, and God can take them away. **BLESSED** is the name of God!"

Job still loved God.

Then God's enemy said, "What if Job was sick? Then he would stop loving You!"

"Let's see if you're right," God said.

BOOM! Satan covered Job with sores, all over! His head hurt, his feet hurt, and everywhere in between hurt. Job was miserable!

Then Job's friends came to visit. They wanted to help Job.

"These terrible things have happened because you've done something terrible," they said. "Tell us what you've done."

But Job replied, "I haven't done **ANYTHING** terrible. I've been following God!"

Job's friends didn't believe him.

"These bad things must be punishment. You need to stop being bad!" they said.

"But I've been **GOOD**!" Job yelled.

Job was getting angry. His friends were getting angry too.

"You are terrible friends!" Job yelled. "And God—why don't You help me out? Why don't You tell them I've been good? You're not being **FAIR**!"

Just then a whirlwind showed up, like a small tornado! And Job and his friends heard a voice. It was God's **VOICE**!

"Who created the seas?" God asked. "Who created the giant animals? Who put the stars in space?" God's voice boomed from the whirlwind. "**AND WHO IS CALLING ME UNFAIR**?"

Job put his hand over his mouth. His whole body was shaking in fear!

Then God turned to Job's friends.

"Just because bad things happened to Job doesn't mean he has been bad. There is more going on than you can see!" God said.

Now Job's friends **SHOOK** with fear!

Did God tell Job about the enemy, who'd said that Job wouldn't love God if bad things happened to him?

No, He didn't.

Why not? Because Job didn't need to **KNOW** everything. Job just needed to trust God. Even when life was **HARD**.

"I have spoken about things I did not understand," Job said. "God **IS** fair."

Then God healed Job's sickness. Job had more kids. And God gave Job more camels, sheep, oxen, and donkeys. **TWICE** as many as he had before!

Job learned that bad things sometimes happen to good people. He also learned that even when life doesn't make sense, God is still in **CONTROL**, and God can still be trusted.

HE GIVES AND TAKES AWAY
FAMILY CONNECTION

JOB 1

TRICKY BITS

Why do bad things happen to good people?

This is one of the trickiest questions about faith! The simple answer is—because we live in a "broken" world. See, when Adam and Eve sinned, God's perfect world became broken. Everything changed! Except God. He is always good and always with us, no matter what.

TALK

Why did Job and his friends think God was being unfair?

When bad things happen, do you get mad or pray and ask God to help you?

Dear God . . .

PRAY

Dear God, thank You for the blessings You give us and even the trials that help us grow. We will trust You, even when bad things happen, because You are good and fair and kind. Amen.

THE BOOK OF SONGS

Did you know there are songs in the

Bible? They're called *psalms,* which means "songs," and there is a whole book filled with them! It's called the book of Psalms, and it has 150 different songs.

There are **HAPPY** psalms for praising God. There are **SAD** psalms that help us bring our troubles to God. There are psalms that celebrate God's law and psalms of **THANKSGIVING**. Psalms about **WISDOM** and psalms about Israel's kings. Lots of psalms!

One of the most popular psalms is Psalm 23. It goes something like this:

God is my **SHEPHERD**. He gives me everything I need.
He lets me rest in beautiful, green pastures.
He lets me drink from cold, fresh streams.
He **REFRESHES** my soul.
He helps me walk on the right paths
so that His **GOODNESS** will be seen.
Even when I walk through dark, scary valleys,
I am **NOT** afraid, because God is with me.
He helps and **DIRECTS** me
with His rod and His staff.
He sets a good meal before me,
EVEN when my enemies are near.
God anoints my head with oil;
My cup is so full it **OVERFLOWS**.
I know for sure God's goodness and love will be with me
for my **ENTIRE** life,
And I will live in God's house **FOREVER**.

Isn't that a beautiful song? It reminds us of God's love. There are many psalms that talk about God's great love.

There are also psalms that help us ask God for **FORGIVENESS** when we've done something wrong.

Once, when King David sinned badly, he wrote a psalm for God that still helps us today. In Psalm 51, David said:

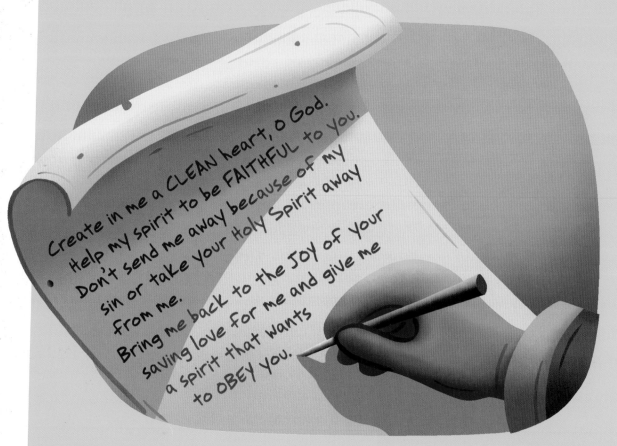

Create in me a CLEAN heart, O God. Help my spirit to be FAITHFUL to you. Don't send me away because of my sin or take your Holy Spirit away from me. Bring me back to the JOY of your saving love for me and give me a spirit that wants to OBEY you.

David knew he couldn't be good all by himself. He needed God's help to do what is **RIGHT**! David knew sometimes he wanted to do bad things. So he asked God to make his heart new and **CLEAN**.

And David asked God to help him feel the joy of God's love for him every day, so he wouldn't want to do bad things.

Psalms is full of songs that express joy *and* sadness, gratitude *and* doubt, pleasure *and* pain. Besides teaching us about God's love and how to worship Him, the psalms remind us it's okay to be **HONEST** with God about all the different ways we feel.

There are 150 psalms in the Bible. Enough songs to read one every time you feel happy, sad, mad, or glad!

THE BOOK OF SONGS
FAMILY CONNECTION

PSALM 23

EVERYDAY TRUTH

God turns my sadness into joy when I talk and sing to Him.

TALK

Dear God . . .

What is your favorite part of Psalm 23?

Why do you think David wrote a psalm to ask God for forgiveness?

PRAY

Dear God, thank You that we can express our feelings to You at any time. Help us turn our sadness into joyful songs as we pray to You. Amen.

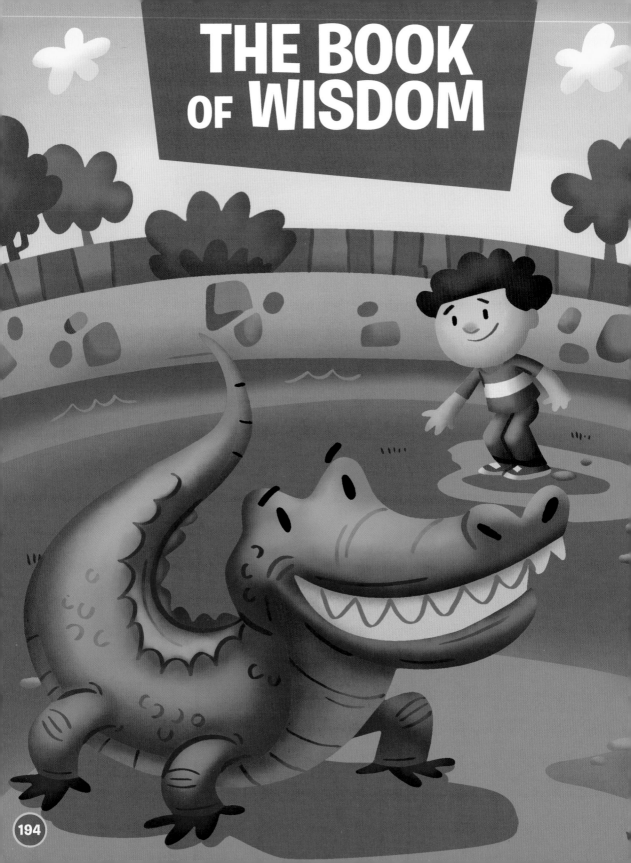

THE BOOK OF WISDOM

Do you know the difference

between being smart and being wise?

To be **SMART** means "to have a lot of knowledge." It means you can solve math problems or you're good at history. We all want to be smart.

Wise means something different. To be **WISE** means "to know how to make good choices in life."

For example, say you know **EVERYTHING** there is to know about alligators. You stand in front of the alligator cage at the zoo and tell everyone what makes alligators special—what they eat, where they come from, how many teeth they have—you have lots of knowledge about alligators! You are smart about alligators.

But then you reach your hand in and try to pet an alligator.

CHOMP!

Not a good choice for your life! You have shown that you have a lot of knowledge about alligators, but you aren't wise about how to act around them. You have **KNOWLEDGE**, but you don't have **WISDOM**.

Remember wisdom from the story of King Solomon?

He asked God for wisdom, and God made him very, very wise. King Solomon wrote lots of wise sayings that were short and easy to remember.

Short, wise sayings are called **PROVERBS**.

King Solomon loved to write proverbs. The Bible says he wrote more than 3,000 of them! And many of those proverbs were collected into a book in the Bible called . . . *guess what?*

Proverbs! Yep, it's a pretty good name for a book full of proverbs!

For gaining wisdom and understanding, for receiving instruction in good living, for doing what is right and **JUST** and fair—this, said Solomon, was the purpose of his proverbs.

Wisdom is like a **TREASURE** more valuable than silver or gold! Solomon wanted everyone to seek wisdom.

Wisdom will **SAVE** you from the ways of wicked people! Wisdom, Solomon believed, would keep you out of trouble.

Here is some other good advice Solomon gave us in Proverbs:

NEVER let love or faithfulness leave you.

TRUST in God with all your heart.

HONOR God with how you spend your money and your time.

Be slow to speak and quick to **LISTEN**.

Don't be a person who likes to fight. Be a **PEACEMAKER**.

LISTEN to good advice!

Don't get **ANGRY** when you are insulted.

WORK HARD and you won't be hungry.

Tell the **TRUTH** and you won't get into trouble.

More than 700 proverbs packed into one book. That's enough to read one each day for nearly two years! Being smart is good. It helps you solve all sorts of problems. But being wise might be even better, because wisdom helps you live a **GOOD** life.

THE BOOK OF WISDOM
FAMILY CONNECTION

PROVERBS

FUN FACTS

There are 915 verses in thirty-one chapters in the book of Proverbs. That's just enough to read one chapter every day for a month! Depending on the translation, the word *wisdom* appears between forty-five and fifty times in the book of Proverbs. No wonder it's called "The Book of Wisdom"!

TALK

What did Solomon say was the purpose of the Proverbs?

Why do you think Solomon said wisdom is more valuable than gold or silver?

Dear God . . .

PRAY

Dear God, we want to be wise so we can live a good life that brings honor to You. Please give us wisdom as we read the Bible and pray. Amen.

THE MESSENGER

When the Israelites were in exile in Babylon, God used a prophet named Isaiah to deliver a very special message.

To be in **EXILE** means you're being "forced to live away from your true home." For the Israelites, their true home was the **PROMISED LAND**, Israel, the land God promised to Abraham and Isaac and Jacob.

God had promised Abraham three things: His family would become a **GREAT** nation, they would have their **OWN** land, and through that nation would come a blessing for the **WHOLE** world!

Those were pretty great promises. But now that Jerusalem was destroyed, and the Israelites were stuck in Babylon, far away from the Promised Land, it seemed like none of those promises were coming true.

Israel was supposed to be a great nation, but now they weren't a nation at all. They had no land. *How could a blessing for the whole world come from Israel now?*

And what about the special promise God made to King David, that one of his family members would sit on the throne of Israel forever? Now there was no throne of Israel!

God's promises confused the Israelites living in Babylon. They wondered if these promises would still come true and if they could still trust God.

God knew how confused they were. So, He sent His prophet **ISAIAH** to give them one of the most **IMPORTANT** messages in the whole Bible.

Is our story **OVER**?" they asked Isaiah. "Is this the **END**?"

"It isn't the end," Isaiah answered. "In fact, just wait until you hear what God is going to do next!"

*Can you **IMAGINE** how excited the Israelites were to hear what Isaiah had to say?*

First, Isaiah told them their time in Babylon wouldn't last forever. Seventy years, he said, and then they would be back in their own land.

Then Isaiah told them about the **MESSIAH**.

Messiah means "anointed one." Samuel had anointed young David with oil as a sign that he was being **SET APART** by God for a very special job—to be king of all Israel!

And now Isaiah was saying that there was another "anointed one" coming. A baby would be born! He would be called **IMMANUEL**, which means "God with us" (but He would also have another name).

This baby would be from King David's family, and He would grow up to rule God's people **FOREVER**!

A forever-kind-of-King, bringing a forever-kind-of-blessing. The blessing for the **WHOLE** world!

How **EXCITED** the Israelites must have been to hear that the story of Israel wasn't over. The promises of God would still come true. Israel would **RETURN** to its land. Someone from King David's family would sit on the throne and be King over God's people—**FOREVER**!

It turns out the hope of the world wasn't a mighty nation or a big army. The hope of the world was a **BABY**!

Can you guess that baby's name?

THE MESSENGER
FAMILY CONNECTION

ISAIAH 9:1-7

EVERYDAY TRUTH

I can wait with hope because God knows what I need.

TALK

Why was it hard for the Israelites to trust God's promises?

What does this story teach us about being patient as we wait on God?

Dear God . . .

PRAY

Dear God, thank You that even when it seems like things aren't going right, we can trust You to bring the blessing we need, right when we need it! Amen.

THE FIERY FURNACE

Nebuchadnezzar was the king of Babylon. He had the biggest army and the biggest empire anyone had ever seen. King Nebuchadnezzar was so powerful, he began to act like he was a god, not a man.

"All the people should bow whenever I say so," he said. So King Nebuchadnezzar built a **GIANT** statue, ninety feet high! That's as tall as a nine-story building! And this statue was covered in **GOLD**! It shone like the sun and could be seen from far away.

"Today I make a new law," said Nebuchadnezzar. "Whenever my musicians play, everyone must **BOW** down to my golden statue!"

"What if they won't bow?" his friends asked.

"Then I will throw them into a blazing hot furnace and **BURN** them up!" Nebuchadnezzar yelled angrily.

This was very bad news for **SHADRACH**, **MESHACH**, and **ABEDNEGO**, three young Israelite men who now lived in Babylon. The friends worked for King Nebuchadnezzar, managing the huge city where they now lived.

"It is time to bow to the golden statue!" announced the king's messengers.

But Shadrach, Meshach, and Abednego **WOULDN'T** bow to the statue. They **WORSHIPPED** the God of Israel, and to bow to any other god—even a pretend god made of wood and gold—would be against God's laws.

When the music played, and everyone in Babylon turned toward the giant statue and bowed down to the ground, Shadrach, Meshach, and Abednego stood up **TALL**. They would not bow.

King Nebuchadnezzar was **FURIOUS**. "You have to bow down, or you will be thrown into the furnace!" he yelled.

"King Nebuchadnezzar," the three men replied, "if you throw us into that furnace, our God can **SAVE** us."

They looked into the hot, hot fire, and then looked back at the king.

"But even if our God doesn't save us from the fire," they said, "we will **NOT** serve your gods **OR** bow down to your statue."

Now the king was even angrier.

"Make the furnace as hot as it can be!" he bellowed. "And throw these men inside!"

The king's guards made the fire hotter. Then they tied up Shadrach, Meshach, and Abednego with ropes and **TOSSED** them into the flames!

And then something strange happened.

King Nebuchadnezzar leaned down and stared into the furnace. His eyes got **BIG**.

Have you ever seen something that you just couldn't **BELIEVE** *you were seeing? Remember how big your eyes got?* King Nebuchadnezzar's eyes got like that, only bigger.

"How many men did we throw into the furnace?" he asked.

"Three!" his guards replied.

The king stared even **HARDER**.

"I see **FOUR** men in the furnace! They're walking around! And the fourth man looks . . ."

King Nebuchadnezzar rubbed his eyes and looked into the furnace again.

"The fourth man looks like a son of the gods!" he said, amazed.

209

Shadrach! Meshach! Abednego!" the king called out. "Come out of the furnace!"

The three men walked out of the furnace. They weren't hurt at **ALL**! Their clothes weren't burnt. Their hair wasn't burnt. They didn't even smell like smoke!

King Nebuchadnezzar couldn't believe what he was seeing. "Your God," he said, "sent an angel to protect you! You trusted your God, and He **SAVED** you from the fire!"

Then the king made a **NEW** law. "From now on, no one can say anything bad about the God of Shadrach, Meshach, and Abednego, because no god is as **STRONG** as their God!"

The most powerful king in the world changed his mind because three friends said, "We're going to follow God, no matter what!"

THE FIERY FURNACE
FAMILY CONNECTION

DANIEL 3

EVERYDAY TRUTH

> When I stand up for God, He is with me and protects me!

TALK

Why do you think Shadrach, Meshach, and Abednego had the courage to stand up for God?

How can you stand up for what you believe about God?

Dear God . . .

PRAY

Dear God, we want to stand up for what we believe about You and trust that You'll protect us. Thank You for giving us the courage to choose Your way! Amen.

DANIEL
AND THE LIONS

Have you ever been to the zoo?
Did you see where they keep the lions? There was probably a big fence or a big glass wall between you and the lions, to keep them from getting out—and to keep **YOU** from falling in!

You don't want to fall in with the lions. Lions are dangerous. To a lion, you look like **LUNCH**!

Long ago, there was a man who fell in with a bunch of lions. Well, he didn't exactly fall in. He was thrown in!

His name was **DANIEL**.

In the time of the exile, when King Nebuchadnezzar had carried the Israelites away to Babylon, some of Israel's smartest young men went to work for the king. We've already learned about three of them—Shadrach, Meshach, and Abednego. They found themselves in a really **HOT** spot because they wouldn't bow down to the king's golden statue.

Daniel was also from Israel. He was smart **AND** wise. He was also a hard worker. When King Nebuchadnezzar had strange dreams, God told Daniel what the dreams meant, and Daniel told the king.

The king was so happy with Daniel that he made him an important **LEADER** in Babylon!

Then King Nebuchadnezzar died, and while Daniel was working for the next king, the Babylonian Empire came to an end. There was a new empire in town—the **PERSIAN** Empire. And a new king! King **DARIUS** of the Persians.

King Darius liked Daniel so much he wanted to put him in charge of the **WHOLE** empire, even though Daniel wasn't Persian! This made some of the Persian leaders mad.

"Why should he be our boss? He isn't even Persian!" they muttered.

The other leaders looked for ways to get Daniel in trouble. But Daniel didn't tell lies, he didn't cheat, and he didn't steal. *How could they get him in trouble if he never did anything wrong?*

Then one of them had a **SNEAKY** idea.

"Daniel is an Israelite, and he prays every day to the God of Israel," he said. "Let's have King Darius make a rule that says for thirty days, **NO ONE** can pray to **ANYONE** except the **KING**!"

The other leaders thought this was a great idea. "And what will happen to people who break the new rule?" they asked.

The guy with the sneaky idea smiled a sneaky smile.

"They'll be **THROWN** into a pit full of **LIONS**!"

Everyone laughed sneaky laughs. Daniel would be lunch for the lions!

Sure enough, their plan worked. King Darius signed the new law. The sneaky guys waited outside Daniel's house to see if they could hear him praying to God.

Daniel could have skipped praying for thirty days. Or he could have prayed in his closet or under his bed, so no one could hear. But he didn't. Daniel **KEPT** praying just the way he always prayed—in his room, with the windows wide-open, looking out toward Jerusalem.

Daniel didn't want to be lunch for the lions. But just like Shadrach, Meshach, and Abednego when they faced the fiery furnace, Daniel knew something important.

God is **BIGGER** than lions.

God is bigger than **ANYTHING** we could possibly face. Daniel didn't want to get thrown to the lions, but he was going to trust God no matter what.

"Daniel is praying to his God!" the sneaky guys told King Darius.

King Darius didn't want Daniel to be lion lunch! But the law was the law.

Very sadly, the king watched as Daniel was thrown into the lions' den. "I hope your God can save you!" he said.

That night, King Darius couldn't sleep. He tossed and turned. He wondered if Daniel's God would protect him. He worried that he'd **NEVER** see his friend again.

In the morning, before the sun was even up, King Darius ran down to the lions' den and rolled back the stone that had kept Daniel **TRAPPED** inside.

"Daniel!" the king yelled. "Are you all right?"

There was silence. Then a voice came from the dark den . . .

"I'm fine! My God shut the mouths of the lions, so they couldn't bite me!"

Daniel was **SAFE**!

King Darius said he would never pass a silly law like that again. And Daniel knew that he could **TRUST** God, because God is bigger than lions!

DANIEL AND THE LIONS
FAMILY CONNECTION

DANIEL 6

TRICKY BITS

What should I do if a grown-up asks me to do something that is against God?

The Bible tells us to respect our leaders, but not every leader in your life will be a follower of God. If a grown-up asks you to do something you feel is against God's ways, share what you believe in a kind way. If you need help, ask an adult you trust, like your parents.

TALK

Dear God . . .

Why do you think Daniel kept praying to God?

What will you do the next time you are faced with a hard choice?

PRAY

Dear God, we want to trust and follow You, no matter what. Give us wisdom and courage when faced with hard choices. Amen.

JONAH AND THE WHALE

You may remember from an earlier story that a prophet was someone who delivered messages for God. Sometimes those messages were **FUN** to deliver. Sometimes they were **NOT** fun to deliver.

Sometimes the prophet was **EXCITED** to deliver his message. Sometimes the prophet was really, really **NOT**.

This is a story about a prophet who was not excited to deliver his message.

His name was **JONAH**.

Jonah lived in the time of the Assyrians. *Remember the Assyrians?* Before the Persians and the Babylonians, the Assyrians ruled the world. They had the **BIGGEST** army and the most **POWERFUL** king. Their capital city, Nineveh, was one of the biggest cities anywhere!

It was also a mean city. The Assyrians were especially mean to their enemies. *And guess who were enemies of the Assyrians?*

Yep. *You guessed it.* The Israelites. To the Israelites, the Assyrians were big, mean bullies. The Israelites really didn't like the Assyrians. At all.

Now, Jonah was a **PROPHET** in Israel. God gave Jonah messages, and Jonah traveled around Israel, delivering them.

Everything was great, until one day God gave Jonah a very strange message.

"Jonah," God said, "I have a message for you to deliver."

"Where to, God?" Jonah asked. "Where in Israel should I go?"

"It's not for Israel," God replied. "It's for Nineveh. I want you to tell them to stop being mean."

Jonah was confused. He wasn't a prophet of **ASSYRIA**! He was a prophet of **ISRAEL**! *And what if the people of Nineveh listened to him? What if they obeyed God? Would God forgive* **THEM**?

That thought made Jonah feel **SICK**. He didn't want God to forgive the Assyrians—they were Israel's enemies!

Jonah didn't know what to do. He just knew he didn't want to do what God wanted him to do! So Jonah ran away.

Since Nineveh was **EAST** of Israel, Jonah decided to go the other way—**WEST**. Far west. As far west as he could possibly go! Jonah jumped on a ship headed to Tarshish, a city all the way across the sea.

Jonah was running from God.

As soon as the ship got out to sea, a **HUGE** storm came! The storm tossed the ship around like a beach ball in a swimming pool, and the sailors were **TERRIFIED**!

"Everyone pray to your gods, so we don't die!" the sailors cried out.

But Jonah was asleep below deck. The captain went down and woke him up.

"Get up and pray to your god, or we'll all **DIE**!" he ordered.

But Jonah couldn't pray to God—he was running from God. Jonah was pretty sure God had sent the storm, and it was because of him.

"It's **MY** fault!" Jonah yelled. "Throw **ME** into the sea and the storm will stop!"

"But you'll die!" the sailors said. Then the storm got even worse, so the sailors grabbed Jonah and **THREW** him into the wild sea.

Jonah could have died. But God wasn't trying to kill Jonah. He was trying to give him a **SECOND CHANCE**. Jonah would be miserable as long as he was running away from God, and God knew it would take something **BIG** to turn Jonah around.

Something as **BIG** as a **WHALE**.

So God sent a whale, and the whale swallowed Jonah!

Now, normally, being eaten by a whale would kill you.

But God **PROTECTED** Jonah in the belly of the whale, and from the belly of the whale, Jonah prayed. He said he was sorry for disobeying God. He asked for a second chance, just like God wanted.

And . . . **PHLOOEY**! The whale spit Jonah up! Right on the beach, safe and sound.

Jonah stood up, brushed himself off, and set off walking to— *can you guess where?*

Yep. Nineveh.

You see, just like Jonah, the people of Nineveh were disobeying God. Just like Jonah, the people of Nineveh were running away from God.

And just like Jonah, the people of Nineveh would get a **SECOND CHANCE**—from God.

Isn't it great to know a God who gives second chances?

JONAH AND THE WHALE
FAMILY CONNECTION

JONAH 1-2

EVERYDAY TRUTH

With God's help, I can obey, even when it's hard!

TALK

Why didn't Jonah want to deliver God's message to Nineveh?

What should we do when God asks us to do something we don't want to do?

Dear God . . .

PRAY

Dear God, we want to obey, even when it's uncomfortable. Give us the strength to always do the right thing according to Your instructions. Amen.

FROM THE OLD TO THE NEW TESTAMENT

The Bible is a book of books divided into two parts: the **OLD TESTAMENT** and the **NEW TESTAMENT**. Together the Old and New Testaments include sixty-six books that tell us God's story, His rescue plan for His people, and how to live as followers of Jesus.

In most Bibles there is only one page between the Old and New Testaments, but really there were **400 YEARS** between the books of Malachi and Matthew. During these 400 years, God was silent. Even still, the people who loved God were waiting with **HOPE** for His third promise to come true!

	OLD	NEW
Books	39	27
Written	1400–400 BC	AD 50-100
Language	Hebrew/Aramaic	Greek
Authors	30	10

"THE GRASS WITHERS AND THE FLOWERS FADE, BUT THE WORD OF OUR GOD STANDS FOREVER." Isaiah 40:8 (NLT)

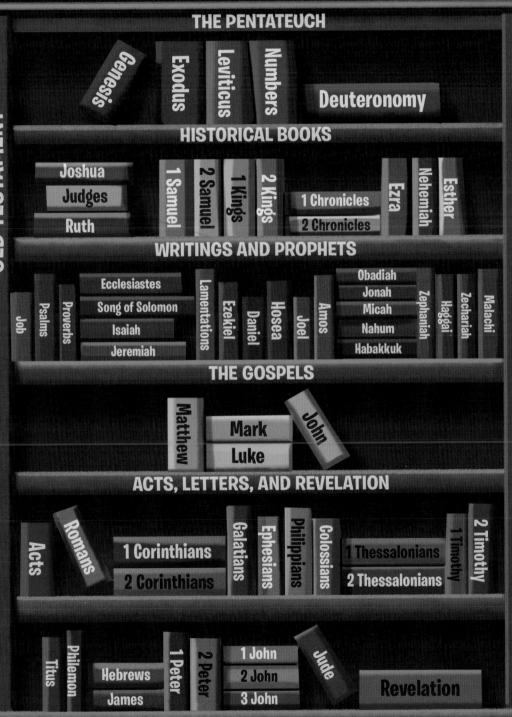

THE PENTATEUCH

Genesis
Exodus
Leviticus
Numbers
Deuteronomy

HISTORICAL BOOKS

Joshua
Judges
Ruth
1 Samuel
2 Samuel
1 Kings
2 Kings
1 Chronicles
2 Chronicles
Ezra
Nehemiah
Esther

WRITINGS AND PROPHETS

Job
Psalms
Proverbs
Ecclesiastes
Song of Solomon
Isaiah
Jeremiah
Lamentations
Ezekiel
Daniel
Hosea
Joel
Amos
Obadiah
Jonah
Micah
Nahum
Habakkuk
Zephaniah
Haggai
Zechariah
Malachi

THE GOSPELS

Matthew
Mark
Luke
John

ACTS, LETTERS, AND REVELATION

Acts
Romans
1 Corinthians
2 Corinthians
Galatians
Ephesians
Philippians
Colossians
1 Thessalonians
2 Thessalonians
1 Timothy
2 Timothy

Titus
Philemon
Hebrews
James
1 Peter
2 Peter
1 John
2 John
3 John
Jude
Revelation

OLD TESTAMENT

NEW TESTAMENT

THE GOSPELS

GOSPEL is another one of those hard-to-understand words, but it just means "**GOOD NEWS**." The gospel is God's rescue plan that we learned about way back at the very beginning of the story, in the Pentateuch. It's God's **RESCUE PLAN** to fix His broken relationship with people. The gospel is the **GOOD NEWS** that Jesus came to die for our sins and give us eternal life with God. So the story of the Gospel books is not just the story of the life of Jesus; it's the story of the **MISSION** of Jesus.

The Gospels give us a picture of **WHO** God is. Because Jesus is God, everything He did while on earth shows us what God is like. Before Jesus died for us, in the first part of His mission, He spent three years preaching and teaching and healing the sick and loving people. **ALL KINDS** of people. Especially people the world had rejected. Especially people who were hurting or lost or scared or in pain or poor or suffering.

Jesus showed us that God is **LOVE**. That God loves **ALL** people. So much that He came to earth to die for them.

"FOR GOD SO LOVED THE WORLD THAT HE GAVE HIS ONE AND ONLY SON . . ." John 3:16 (NIV)

THE GOSPELS

Matthew | Mark | Luke | John

The Old Testament pointed ahead to Jesus as the **ONLY WAY** to fix our broken relationship with God. In the Gospels, we meet Jesus. Jesus Himself says:

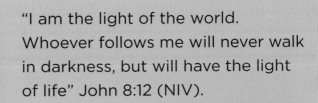

"I am the light of the world. Whoever follows me will never walk in darkness, but will have the light of life" John 8:12 (NIV).

"I am the good shepherd [who] lays down his life . . . " John 10:11 (NIV).

"I am the way and the truth and the life. No one comes to the Father except through me" John 14:6 (NIV).

THE FAMILY OF JESUS

Did you know we can trace Jesus' family all the way back to Abraham? Remember God's third promise? "From your family will come a blessing for the whole world."

Jesus was the blessing, and His family history (or genealogy) shows God's faithfulness to do what He promised—no matter how long it took!

A **GENEALOGY** is the line of people traced down from one generation to the next.

A **GENERATION** includes all of the people who are born and live around the same time. You and all of your friends are a generation. Your parents are from another generation.

A **DESCENDANT** is someone who is part of your family and is born after you. So your "descendants" would be your children, your grandchildren, your great-grandchildren, and so on.

"FOR TO US A CHILD IS BORN, TO US A SON IS GIVEN . . .
HE WILL REIGN ON DAVID'S THRONE AND OVER HIS KINGDOM . . .
FROM THAT TIME ON AND FOREVER." Isaiah 9:6–7 (NIV)

ABRAHAM

Abraham was the father of Isaac. Isaac was the father of Jacob (aka Israel). Jacob had twelve sons *(remember Joseph?),* including one named Judah. Judah had kids, and then they had kids, and, well... you remember how this goes . . .

11 GENERATIONS

BOAZ

Boaz was the son of Salmon (no, not the fish!) and the great-great-great-great-great-great-grandson of Judah. *Remember Boaz?* He married Ruth and redeemed her family.

3 GENERATIONS

DAVID

David was the son of Jesse and the great-grandson of Boaz. Remember, God promised King David that one of his "descendants" would be King forever—the blessing for the whole world! But David had to trust God, because he wouldn't be around to see the promise fulfilled.

26 GENERATIONS

Joseph was the son of Jacob. No, not Isaac's son Jacob. Lots of people were named Jacob back then—and today too! Joseph was a carpenter. He led a simple and humble life, which is probably why God chose Joseph to be Jesus' dad.

JOSEPH

1 GENERATION

JESUS

There were forty-one generations between the time God made His promises to Abraham and when the last promise came true through the birth of Jesus—the Savior of the world. That's almost 2,000 years of trusting God! But Jesus was well worth the wait!

BORN IN A BARN

Remember Abraham?

God gave him three promises.

1. YOUR CHILDREN WILL BECOME A GREAT NATION.

2. THAT NATION WILL HAVE ITS OWN LAND.

3. FROM THAT NATION WILL COME A BLESSING FOR THE WHOLE WORLD.

After 1,500 years, two of those promises had come true. Abraham's kids became the nation of Israel, and they got their own land. The Promised Land.

But the blessing for the WHOLE world? WHAT was it? And WHEN was it coming? Would it solve the problem of sin? Would it change the people of the world, so they could be friends with God again?

The prophet Isaiah talked about the "Messiah," a word that means "ANOINTED ONE." God anointed kings and very special leaders when He had an important job for them to do.

But 400 years had passed since the time of Isaiah—400 years without any new prophets . . . 400 years without any new messages from God—and the Israelites were getting tired of waiting for this special leader.

WHERE was the blessing?

Some of the Israelites were starting to lose hope.

But THEN something incredible happened.

An angel appeared to a young woman named Mary.

"You will have a son!" the angel said.

"How will this be?" Mary asked. "I'm not even married!"

It's true—Mary wasn't married. She had promised to marry a man named Joseph. But they weren't married yet. Then the angel said something amazing. He told Mary the baby's father would be **GOD** Himself! Her baby would be the **SON** of **GOD**!

Pretty wild, right? You would think that Mary would have passed out and fallen on the floor right then! But Mary was brave. She trusted God.

"I am the servant of the Lord," she said. "May this happen just as you have said."

Then the angel said one more thing to Mary. He said the baby's name would be **JESUS**.

When it was almost time for the baby to come, Joseph and Mary traveled to Bethlehem. They needed somewhere to stay—a nice place for Mary to have her baby.

If this baby really was God's own son, He should be born in a palace, right? In a **BIG**, beautiful palace, surrounded by fancy people wearing fancy clothes! After all, this baby was the Son of God!

But Mary didn't have her baby in a fancy palace. Or in a nice, warm inn, by a fire. No, Mary had her baby in a barn for animals. Mary's baby—Jesus—wasn't surrounded by fancy people. He was surrounded by sheep. And goats. And chickens.

If this was God's blessing for the **WORLD**—the blessing Israel had been awaiting for almost 2,000 years—this wasn't the way people expected it to happen!

Then more angels showed up. A whole bunch of them! And they sang and celebrated the birth of a new king! The birth of Jesus!

Where do you think God's mighty angels announced the birth of His Son? Probably in the biggest city, to the world's most important people, right? To kings and generals! To rich, important, fancy people!

But that isn't where the angels sang of Jesus' birth. This amazing group of God's **MESSENGERS** appeared in the middle of a field. In the middle of nowhere. And they didn't sing to kings and rich folks. They sang to shepherds. To a group of dirty, smelly guys who took care of dirty, smelly sheep.

God showed the world His power—who He really was—not in an army, but in a baby. Not in a palace, but in a stable. Not to kings and rich people, but to **SHEPHERDS**.

God's rescue plan was happening. His kingdom was on the move. But God was announcing, very clearly, that this blessing for the world wasn't going to be what people expected.

This little tiny baby, born in a stable, celebrated by shepherds, was going to turn the whole world upside down!

BORN IN A BARN
FAMILY CONNECTION

LUKE 2:1-21

FUN FACTS

The "crib" used to hold Baby Jesus after His birth is called a manger. The word *manger* comes from the Latin word *mandere*, meaning "to chew" and the French *manger*, meaning, "to eat." A manger was a feeder for animals such as donkeys, cattle, and horses. The Bible tells us that Jesus was placed in a manger because there was no room for His family at the inn (Luke 2:7).

TALK

In what ways was Jesus' arrival different than people expected?

What do you think God was trying to show the world by sending His Son this way?

Dear God . . .

PRAY

Dear God, thank You for sending Your Son, Jesus, as a blessing for the whole world. Help us to trust You when your blessing looks different than we expected. Amen.

JOHN BAPTIZES JESUS

John is a popular name, isn't it?

There are lots of people named John! There are two very famous Johns in the Bible.

The first famous John is John the disciple. He was one of Jesus' closest friends. He also wrote five different books in the Bible!

The other famous John is **JOHN THE BAPTIST**. John the Baptist was a relative of Jesus. He was six months older than Jesus. We call John "the Baptist" because he baptized people. That means he dunked people in water—usually a river or stream—as a **SIGN** that they wanted to have their sin "washed" away. Even today, being baptized shows that a person wants to live for God!

If you met John the Baptist, you'd probably think to yourself, *This guy is a little weird.* John the Baptist wasn't like most Israelites. He didn't dress like they did. Instead of clothes made from soft wool or cotton, John the Baptist made his clothes from itchy camel hair.

Instead of eating the food most folks ate, John ate only **HONEY** (yum!) and **BUGS** (yuck!).

And John didn't live in one of the towns of Israel like everyone else. John lived out in the wilderness, all by himself. Yep, John the Baptist was a little unusual.

John spent his days walking around in his itchy camel clothes, preaching about the kingdom of God and the Messiah.

"Stop doing BAD things!" he'd yell. "The day of God is coming!"

Soon people from towns and villages started coming out to see this bug-eating guy in itchy camel clothes, who said he had a message from God.

"Is this a new prophet?" they wondered. Israel hadn't had a new prophet in 400 years!

"Maybe he is the Messiah!" someone said.

But John shook his head. "I'm not the Messiah. He is coming—someone so great that I don't even deserve to touch His SHOES!"

People were amazed. This bug-eating, camel-clothed guy seemed like he was really close to God! *Who could be coming that was even closer?*

By now, Jesus was around thirty years old, but the people didn't know who He was. One day Jesus came to John and said, "Baptize me!"

John was confused. He knew who Jesus was. He knew that Jesus had never done anything wrong. It seemed to him that Jesus should baptize John, not the other way around!

But Jesus said, "No, it is right for you to baptize Me."

So John baptized Jesus in the river, and when Jesus came up out of the water, something AMAZING happened.

First, something that looked like a dove came down from the sky and landed on Jesus!

It was the **SPIRIT** of God!

Then a voice came out of the air and said, "This is my Son, whom I love very much. I am very happy with Him!"

It was the **VOICE** of God!

People couldn't believe what they had seen and heard. The Spirit of God came to rest on this fellow they'd never heard of. This Jesus. And God Himself had spoken out loud about Him!

Who was Jesus? Was He the Messiah they had been waiting on for so long? Was this finally God's blessing for the world?

No one knew for sure, but they went home that day very excited!

JOHN BAPTIZES JESUS
FAMILY CONNECTION

TRICKY BITS

What is baptism?

Baptism can be done by sprinkling water on the forehead (infant baptism) or as John performed, by full immersion in water (getting dunked). Being immersed in water and raised up again represents the cleansing that occurs when we accept God's gift of salvation. Because of Jesus, we can have a fresh, new life!

- We baptize to declare our new life in Jesus (Romans 6:4).
- We baptize to follow Jesus' example (Luke 3:21–22).
- We baptize because Jesus told us to (Matthew 28:19).

TALK

What made John the Baptist stand out from the crowd?

Why do you think Jesus asked John to baptize Him?

Dear God . . .

PRAY

Dear God, we want to stand out for You like John the Baptist did. Please show us how to boldly point people to You. Amen.

THE DESERT TEMPTATION

After Jesus was baptized, He did something unusual.

The crowd around John the Baptist was very excited. They had seen the Holy Spirit appear like a dove and had heard the voice of God calling Jesus His **SON**! Maybe the Messiah—the One who would save Israel and bless the whole world—was finally here!

It was the perfect time for Jesus to say, "Okay, everybody, follow Me! I'm the Messiah!"

But He didn't. Instead, Jesus walked off into the wilderness, all by Himself. He left the crowds behind and went out into the wildest parts of Israel to be **ALONE**.

You see, Jesus knew what was coming. He knew that being the Messiah—that saving Israel and blessing the world—was going to be very, very hard. He knew He couldn't do it unless He was very close to God, His Father.

So Jesus went off to spend time with His **DAD**.

243

For forty days Jesus stayed in the wilderness. He didn't eat any food. He spent all of His time talking with God, His Father.

At the end of forty days, Jesus and His Dad were very, very close. But He was also very, **VERY** hungry.

And then Jesus had a visitor.

Do you know who it was? It was that sneaky **SNAKE**, God's enemy, the one who had lied to Adam and Eve way back at the beginning so sin would ruin God's world.

God's enemy knew Jesus was hungry. He knew the big things Jesus had to do would be hard. God's enemy showed up to **TEMPT** Jesus with ways to make things easier.

"If You really are God's Son," the enemy said, "why don't You just turn these rocks into bread? Then You can eat!"

"No," Jesus said. "I don't live by bread, I live by the words that come from My Father."

Then the enemy took Jesus to the **HIGHEST** place in Jerusalem— the very top of the temple.

"Jump off!" he said. "God will send angels to save You, and then everyone will be impressed, and they'll want to follow You!"

But Jesus replied, "That is not God's plan. Don't test God with tricks."

Finally, the enemy took Jesus to the top of a high mountain. Jesus could see **ALL** the kingdoms of the world.

"Do You want to rule all these kingdoms?" the enemy asked. "I can make that happen! All You have to do is bow down and worship **ME**."

What should Jesus do? God wanted Jesus to be a new kind of king. A blessing for the whole world! Jesus knew that God's plan was going to be very, very hard. God's enemy said he could make it easy. *Wouldn't that be better?*

245

But Jesus knew He was talking to a **LIAR**.

"I will only bow to God!" Jesus yelled. "Leave me now!"

And the enemy left. He had tried his best to fool Jesus, the same way he had fooled Adam and Eve many years before. But Jesus was too close to God, His Father. And being close to His Father made Jesus strong.

God took care of Jesus, because He was God's Son, and God loved Him very much.

NOW it was time to save the world.

THE DESERT TEMPTATION
FAMILY CONNECTION

MATTHEW 4:1-11

TRICKY BITS

If Jesus is God, how could He be tempted?

This is a tricky question, all right! Jesus was God, but Philippians 2:7 (ICB) says He "gave up his place with God and made himself nothing" to carry out God's rescue plan. God's enemy wanted to see if Jesus would follow through. He wanted Jesus to act in God's power and step outside God's plan. But Jesus passed the test! He resisted the temptation, humbling Himself to become the blessing for the whole world.

TALK

What was Jesus doing when God's enemy came to tempt Him?

How should we respond when we are tempted by God's enemy?

Dear God . . .

PRAY

Dear God, thank You for giving us the power to overcome temptation and choose Your way! Amen.

THE PHONY PHARISEES

Jesus was traveling around Israel, teaching people about the kingdom of God. And people were amazed! They'd never heard anyone teach like Jesus did. Then Jesus started doing things that were even MORE amazing. He started healing people. People who were sick. People who couldn't see. People who couldn't walk. Jesus would simply touch them, or just say one word, and they were healed!

If someone came to your house who could make sick people better or make blind people see just by touching them, you'd be pretty excited, right? You'd probably tell all your friends about it.

Well, that's what happened with Jesus. People told their friends about the things they saw Jesus do, and those people told **THEIR** friends . . . and pretty soon everywhere Jesus went, hundreds of people were showing up to see Him.

Including the **PHARISEES**.

Who were the Pharisees? In Jesus' day, the Israelites hung out in different groups. Sort of like at school, where you might have the kids who are good at sports, and the kids who are good at science, and the kids who are good at music.

Well, the Pharisees were the people who were REALLY good at following rules. *Remember all the rules God gave Moses way back at Mount Sinai? Remember the Ten Commandments?* Those rules. The Pharisees loved following them.

The Pharisees even made up MORE rules. Rules for how to dress, what to eat, how to sell and buy things. Who to eat with. How to wash their hands. Rules about everything! They were more concerned with following the rules than following God.

When the Pharisees heard about this guy named Jesus who was doing amazing things and attracting big crowds of people, they only had one question: *Is He following all the rules?*

The Pharisees started watching Jesus to see what He would do.

Healing people? That was okay . . . **UNLESS** He healed them on Saturday! Saturday was the Sabbath, and the law of Moses said no one should work on the Sabbath.

Eating dinner with people? That was fine . . . **UNLESS** He didn't wash His hands the right way first, or He ate with people who did bad things, like tax collectors, who always took more than they were supposed to from people.

Sure enough, Jesus healed someone on a Saturday. He broke a **RULE**! And then He ate dinner with a tax collector. Another broken rule!

Jesus knew the Pharisees were watching Him, so He did something **REALLY** wild.

There was a man who couldn't walk. He needed to be healed. But instead of healing him, Jesus said, "Your sins are forgiven."

The Pharisees went nuts!

Why did the Pharisees go nuts? Because forgiving sins was something only God could do. If Jesus thought **HE** could forgive sins, that meant Jesus thought He was equal to God!

Saying you were equal to God was just about the biggest rule you could break. In fact, the punishment for breaking that rule was **DEATH**!

Jesus knew what the Pharisees were thinking. So He looked at them, right in the eyes, and said, "What is easier? To say to this man, 'Your sins are forgiven,' or to say, 'Get up and walk'? If you don't think I can forgive sins, watch this."

And Jesus turned to the man and said, "Get up and walk!"

THE PHONY PHARISEES
FAMILY CONNECTION

MATTHEW 9:1-8

EVERYDAY TRUTH

God helps me live out what I believe.

TALK

Dear God . . .

Why did the Pharisees have a problem with Jesus?

In what ways can we sometimes act like the Pharisees today?

PRAY

Dear God, we don't want to be Pharisees! Help us to live Your way in our attitude and actions. Amen.

JESUS' DISCIPLES

The kingdom of God is here!

Repent and believe the good news!"

Jesus walked around Israel and said this to everyone He met.

What is the "KINGDOM OF GOD"? The kingdom of God is where God rules. It's anywhere—in heaven or on earth—where what God wants to happen is happening.

What does it mean to "repent"? It means to turn away from the bad things we used to do. To put those bad things away and leave them behind.

And what was this "GOOD NEWS"?

Well, that part is simple. The good news is Jesus!

Jesus, the Son of God, the Messiah, was here at last! The promises from long, long ago, made to Abraham and Isaac and Jacob and David, were finally coming true. Many of the Israelites knew all the old stories about Abraham and Moses. They remembered Isaiah's promises about the coming of a NEW king—the Messiah!

It was time for God to reveal what He had always wanted to happen—right before their eyes!

Some of them were very excited when they saw Jesus.

"This could be Him! This could be the Messiah!"

Others were confused.

"This could be the Messiah?" they wondered.

You see, many Israelites thought the Messiah would be a great military leader. In Jesus' day, Israel was a part of the Roman Empire. The Roman Empire was bigger than the Assyrian Empire. Bigger than the Babylonian Empire. Even bigger than the Persian Empire! The Israelites couldn't do ANYTHING unless the Romans said it was okay.

This really bothered some of the Israelites.

"When the Messiah comes," they'd say to each other, "He's going to kick the Romans out of Israel! We'll have our OWN nation again!"

But Jesus didn't look like that kind of Messiah. He wasn't dressed like a warrior, or riding a big horse, or carrying a sword. He just looked like . . . a guy. A REGULAR guy. He didn't have a horse. He didn't even have a donkey!

"This could be the Messiah?" they asked.

Then Jesus did something interesting. He started collecting PEOPLE. First, two brothers named Simon and Andrew. Simon and Andrew were fishermen.

"Follow Me," Jesus said.

And they did. They put down their fishing nets, and they followed Jesus.

Then two more fishermen, James and John. They got right out of their boat and followed Jesus. Then a tax collector named Levi. Nobody liked tax collectors, because they often cheated people. But Jesus chose Levi anyway. He looked at Levi, a guy no one liked, and said, "Follow Me."

And Levi did.

Jesus kept collecting people—Philip, Bartholomew, Matthew, Thomas, another James, Thaddeus, another Simon, and Judas.

TWELVE people in all.

You will be my disciples," He said.

What's a **DISCIPLE**? A disciple is a student. But in Jesus' day, a disciple didn't just go to class with his teacher. He **LIVED** with his teacher! Disciples learned how to live good lives by watching their teacher.

"I will teach you how to live your life," Jesus said to His disciples. "But not just any kind of life. The forever-kind-of-life in the kingdom of God!"

A kind of life no one had been able to live because sin had broken God's creation. Jesus was going to teach that kind of life to His new students—to His new friends!

"And what will we do after we start living this kind of life?" they wondered.

Jesus smiled.

"Teach it to the **WHOLE** world."

Jesus was bringing a new kind of life to His disciples. A forever-kind-of-life. And these twelve people—fishermen and tax collectors, ordinary people—were going to teach it to the world!

JESUS' DISCIPLES
FAMILY CONNECTION

LUKE 5:1-11

EVERYDAY TRUTH

I am a disciple of Jesus, choosing to follow His way, every day!

TALK

What is a *disciple*?

In what ways are we God's disciples?

Dear God . . .

PRAY

Dear God, we want to follow You and tell Your good news to others. Thank You for trusting us to share Your love with the world. Amen.

THE SERMON ON THE MOUNT

Blessed are the poor in spirit.

The kingdom of God belongs to them."

Jesus was standing on a hill, and a huge crowd had gathered to hear Him talk.

"Blessed are those who are sad. They will be comforted."

Jesus was making a list, but it wasn't a kind of list that **ANYONE** had heard before.

"Blessed are those who don't put themselves first. They will receive the whole world."

Jesus was listing people who didn't have much. People who were sad. People who didn't use their strength to get their own way. People who tried to make peace when other people were fighting, and probably got punched right in the jaw because of it.

Jesus was listing people who **USUALLY** ended up at the back of the line.

"Not anymore," He said. "In the kingdom of God, you will be the happiest of them all!"

Whoa.

Jesus was talking about God's kingdom—where God is in control—and it sounded like an **UPSIDE-DOWN** world!

If you've been sad, you'll be happy. If you've been last, you'll be first. If you've tried to make peace, you will be the sons and daughters of the King of Peace. The sons and daughters of God Himself!

The people around Jesus couldn't believe what they were hearing. The least important people in the kingdoms of earth will be the **MOST** important in the kingdom of God?

Remember how the angels brought the message of Jesus' birth not to kings and rich people, but to shepherds? Remember how Jesus was born not in a palace, but in a barn?

Yep. God's kingdom is totally different from the kingdoms of earth! But Jesus wasn't finished.

"The law of Moses says to not kill people," He said. "But I say, hating someone in your heart is JUST as bad!"

What? Hating someone is as bad as killing them?

"The law says people who hurt you should be punished. But I say, if someone hits you on the cheek, let them hit your other cheek too. If someone steals your shirt, give them your coat as well!"

What? Give my coat to someone who steals my shirt?

"The law says to love your neighbors. But I say you should love your enemies just as much!"

People got REALLY confused.

"This guy is crazy!" they said to each other.

But Jesus wasn't crazy. Jesus was teaching them about a whole new way to live. A forever-kind-of-life lived with God.

You see, the old rules of Moses could only change what you did on the OUTSIDE. They couldn't change who you were on the INSIDE.

I didn't come to make you do better things," Jesus said. "I came to make you **DIFFERENT** people. I came to make you the kind of person that I am."

And that kind of person doesn't need all those rules. That kind of person has a new heart. A heart that loves everyone. A heart that gives to everyone. A heart that puts other people first, always. A heart like Jesus' heart.

"Come to me, all you who are tired, worn-out, and weighed down by the rules. I'm not here to make you follow the rules. I'm here to make you a new person!"

Standing on the hill that day, preaching his "Sermon on the Mount," Jesus invited everyone into a new kind of life. A life that wasn't about rules, but about **RELATIONSHIP**. A life that was about a relationship with Jesus that can change us from the inside out!

THE SERMON ON THE MOUNT
FAMILY CONNECTION

MATTHEW 5

EVERYDAY TRUTH

My relationship with Jesus helps me live God's way.

TALK

What did Jesus come to do according to this sermon?

If it's not about rules, what is our new life with Jesus about?

Dear God . . .

PRAY

Dear God, thank You that Jesus provides a way for us to be in relationship with You again. Thank You for our new life in Christ. Amen.

IT'S A MIRACLE!

Jesus and His disciples walked all over Israel. Everywhere they went, big crowds would gather to see Jesus.

He talked a lot about the kingdom of God. But He didn't just **TALK** about the kingdom of God; Jesus also **SHOWED** people what the kingdom of God was like.

How? By doing amazing things. Unbelievable things! Jesus called them "signs" that pointed to the kingdom of God. Today we call them **MIRACLES**.

In Jesus' day, many people were **AFRAID** of the sea. Fishermen and sailors had to go out on the sea, which often put them in danger. Today we have satellites that tell sailors when big storms are headed their way, but back in Jesus' day, it was hard to know when a big storm was coming. The sea was scary!

One night, Jesus was on a boat with His disciples when a **HUGE** storm took over the sea. Their boat was going to sink, and the disciples were afraid they would die. Meanwhile, Jesus was asleep in the boat.

The disciples woke up Jesus and said, "Hey! Did You notice the storm? We're going to die!"

Jesus opened His eyes, looked at them, and said, "Why are you so afraid?"

Then He turned to the storm—the **GIANT** storm that was sinking their boat—and said, "Stop it!"

And guess what? The storm stopped! Completely.

The disciples couldn't believe what had just happened. *Who can talk to a storm and the storm obeys Him?*

Jesus was giving them a **SIGN**. In the kingdom of God, there was no danger from the sea, because Jesus was the King of everything! Even the big, scary sea listened to Jesus.

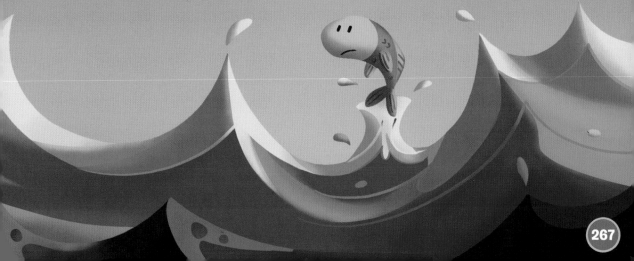

nother time Jesus was surrounded by thousands of people who had followed Him far away from town with no food to eat.

The disciples got nervous. "What will we give them to eat?" they wondered.

One little boy had **TWO** loaves of bread and **FIVE** small fish. He gave them to the disciples.

"Will this help?" he said.

The disciples thought it was silly. You can't feed thousands of people with two loaves of bread and five little fish!

Or can you?

Jesus took the boy's gift and prayed over it. Then He started breaking pieces off and giving them to people.

And there were more pieces . . .

And more pieces . . .

And **MORE** pieces . . .

So many pieces that every person got to eat as much as they wanted. The disciples couldn't believe their eyes!

"Why are you so surprised?" Jesus asked.

He was giving them another sign. In the kingdom of God, there is **ALWAYS** enough. Enough food, enough warmth, enough love. Where Jesus is King, we will never run out of anything!

Jesus also **HEALED** people. This was a sign that Jesus was King over sickness and disease. In the kingdom of God, there is no sickness!

But even more amazing, one time when a sick little girl died before Jesus could get there to heal her, Jesus said to her parents, "Don't worry. She's okay."

And the little girl came back to life, got up, and walked **RIGHT** out of her room! Even though she had died. Even death has to obey Jesus in the kingdom of God.

Everyone was amazed by the things Jesus did. The crowds that followed Him got bigger, and bigger, and **BIGGER**. Everyone was excited to see Jesus!

Except the Pharisees. *Remember them?* They thought Jesus was getting **TOO** popular. **TOO** many people were following Him around, and some of those people even said they thought Jesus should be king!

The Pharisees went to the Sadducees to talk about Jesus.

Who were the Sadducees? They were the group of Israelites who were in charge of punishments. The Pharisees kept track of all the rules, and the Sadducees were in charge of **PUNISHING** the people who broke the rules.

"This Jesus guy is breaking rules and causing trouble!" said the Pharisees.

Hmm, thought the Sadducees, *We might have to do something about that.*

So the Sadducees began looking for a way to arrest Jesus.

IT'S A MIRACLE!
FAMILY CONNECTION

MARK 4:35-41; MARK 6:30-44; MARK 5:21-43

FUN FACTS

There are thirty-seven miracles of Jesus recorded in the Gospels. Jesus healed someone twenty-four times, He performed a miracle of nature ten times, and He raised someone from the dead three times! The Feeding of the 5,000 is the only miracle recorded in all of the Gospels (Matthew, Mark, Luke, and John).

TALK

What do Jesus' miracles tell us about the kingdom of God?

Have you ever experienced a miracle?

Dear God . . .

PRAY

Dear God, we are thankful for Your miraculous power. Help us trust You to do miracles even today. Amen.

THE LAST SUPPER

Jesus and His disciples walked to Jerusalem to celebrate Passover.

What was Passover?

Remember when God rescued the Israelites from Egypt by sending plagues of frogs and flies and darkness? Remember the angel God sent to kill the firstborn sons of the Egyptians, when Pharaoh refused to let the Israelites go free? That angel "passed over" the homes of the Israelites if they had the blood of a LAMB over their doors. The sons of Israel were saved by the blood of that lamb.

Ever since that day, Israelites have celebrated Passover with a SPECIAL meal, just like the one they had that night in Egypt many years earlier. So Jesus and His disciples traveled to Jerusalem for Passover. Lots of other people came, too, and many of them had heard stories about Jesus.

As Jesus rode into Jerusalem on a donkey, a big crowd of people came out to meet Him. They laid down palm branches in front of Him, which was a sign of royalty. They shouted, "Blessed is He who comes in the name of the Lord!" and "Blessed is the coming kingdom of David!" It was like a parade for a KING.

This made the Pharisees and Sadducees **VERY** nervous. Since Israel was a part of the Roman Empire, the Israelites weren't allowed to have their own king. The king of the Romans was Israel's king. Any time someone in Israel said, "Let's have a new king," the Romans would send in soldiers and throw a bunch of people in **PRISON**—or worse!

The Pharisees and Sadducees had to do something to stop all the commotion about Jesus and this talk of a "new king." And they had to do it fast! *But what could they do?*

Jesus and His disciples got together to eat the Passover meal, just like they did every year. But this year, Jesus did something **DIFFERENT**.

First, Jesus told His disciples that **ONE** of them was going to turn against Him by helping the Pharisees and Sadducees arrest Him and take Him away!

All the disciples looked at each other. "Who could it be?" they wondered.

Then Jesus picked up a piece of **BREAD** and said, "This is My body, which is given for you."

After that, He picked up His **CUP**, and said, "This cup is the new covenant of My blood, poured out for you."

A **COVENANT** is a "promise," like the promises that God had made to Abraham long, long before.

The disciples were confused. It sounded like Jesus was saying God was making a new promise—a new way to bless them and save them—and it had something to do with Jesus' blood and body. It had something to do with Jesus . . . dying?

The disciples couldn't believe their ears. *Was Jesus saying that He was the new Passover lamb? That He was going to die to save them? But* **HOW** *could Jesus be king if He wasn't even alive?*

Everyone was confused.

After dinner, Jesus went out to a garden to **PRAY**. He knew what He had to do next, and He knew it wasn't going to be easy.

When He finished praying, Jesus turned to His friends and said, "The hour has come."

And just at that moment, His disciple Judas walked into the garden, leading a group of soldiers sent by the Sadducees to arrest Jesus.

THE LAST SUPPER
FAMILY CONNECTION

MATTHEW 21:1-11;
MATTHEW 26:17-50

TRICKY BITS

WHAT is Communion? Communion is a symbolic practice of the Last Supper message of Jesus.

WHO can take Communion? Followers of Jesus.

WHAT do we take? A piece of bread, to represent Jesus' body, broken for us. A cup of wine, to represent His blood, shed for us.

WHY do we take it? To remember Jesus' sacrifice.

TALK

What *covenant* or "promise" did Jesus make to His disciples during their Passover meal?

What do you think it means that Jesus was the new Passover lamb?

Dear God . . .

PRAY

Dear God, thank You for the hope we have because Jesus was willing to be our Passover lamb. Amen.

The soldiers who arrested Jesus

brought him to the Pharisees and Sadducees.

"You think You are equal to God?" they asked Him. But Jesus wouldn't say anything.

The Pharisees didn't care if He answered or not. "Guilty!" they shouted. "He is guilty of blasphemy!"

And the penalty for BLASPHEMY—for saying you are equal to God?

DEATH.

There was a problem, though. Even if the Pharisees and Sadducees said Jesus was guilty, they weren't allowed to kill anyone. Only the Romans could do that. So they dragged Jesus to the Roman governor, Pontius Pilate.

Pontius Pilate looked at Jesus and asked, "What have You done that has made everyone so angry?"

But still, Jesus wouldn't say **ANYTHING**.

"I don't see anything wrong with this man!" Pilate said to the Pharisees and Sadducees.

But they all yelled back, "According to our rules, He needs to die!"

Pilate didn't know what to do. He didn't think Jesus deserved to **DIE**, but he didn't want the Pharisees and Sadducees to complain about him to the other Roman leaders. Staying out of trouble was the best way to keep your job as a Roman governor. Maybe the troublemaker had to go.

So Pilate gave in. He washed his hands in front of the crowd, which was a way of saying, "This isn't my fault."

Then he had Jesus killed on a wooden CROSS.

As Jesus was dying, He looked up to heaven and said, "Father, forgive them. They don't know what they are doing." Even at that moment, Jesus was forgiving. Even at that moment, He was loving.

The sky turned DARK. Jesus died. Then the ground began to SHAKE! A Roman guard standing near Jesus saw everything that happened and said, "This man must have been the Son of God!"

But it was too late. Jesus was dead.

Jesus' friends didn't know what to think. *How could Jesus be the Messiah, the blessing for the whole world, if He wasn't even alive?*

Jesus had done some AMAZING things while He was living. He'd shown everyone what God the Father was like. Incredibly loving. Incredibly good. Incredibly powerful. The life of Jesus had taught people who God is.

Jesus had also announced the KINGDOM OF GOD. Before Adam and Eve sinned, they'd lived with God, the way things were supposed to be. There was no sickness, no hunger, no hurting, and no death.

Jesus had said the kingdom of God was back. He'd given everyone a taste of that kingdom through His miracles. Jesus showed us that in this kingdom of God, there is nothing to be afraid of—not even death!

Jesus also explained that the kingdom was starting small, like a seed. Jesus' miracles were like tiny green shoots from a seed, poking up through the soil. Those shoots would grow bigger and bigger, until finally the day would come when Jesus is King, and the kingdom of God would be EVERYWHERE! When the whole world would be made new again, the way God always wanted it to be!

But what about sin? What about the selfish and mean things we do that keep us far from God? Did Jesus do anything about that?

He sure did. As Jesus was dying on the cross, God saw all the bad things we've ever done, the **STAIN** of our sin, appear on Jesus. Jesus became "dirty" with all that sin so that we would have a chance to be clean. So that we could be with God again.

Jesus died so we wouldn't have to. Jesus died so we could live with God in a world without sin, without sickness, without death. A world where Jesus is King.

You're probably asking: *If Jesus died, how can He be King?*

That's a good question—with an even better answer.

Because Jesus didn't **STAY** dead!

JESUS' DEATH
FAMILY CONNECTION

MATTHEW 27:32-54

EVERYDAY TRUTH

I live because Jesus Christ died for me!

TALK

Why did Jesus die on the cross?

What happened to the "stain" of our sin when He died?

Dear God . . .

PRAY

Dear God, thank You for sending Your Son, Jesus, to die on the cross for our sins. Help us to live with Him as the King of our lives. Amen.

HE IS ALIVE!

There was a rich man named Joseph from a town called Arimathea. He wasn't the same Joseph that was married to Jesus' mother, Mary, or the Joseph with the coat of many colors. Joseph was a popular name back then.

Joseph was a **FOLLOWER** of Jesus. He loved Jesus. Like all of Jesus' followers, Joseph was very sad when Jesus died. He wanted to do something nice for Jesus, to show how much he **LOVED** Him.

So Joseph went to Pontius Pilate, the Roman governor, and asked if he could take care of Jesus' body. And Pontius Pilate said yes.

When important people died in Israel, they weren't buried in the ground. Instead, their bodies were placed in special TOMBS that were carved out of solid rock, like small caves. Joseph had a special tomb that he had made to use when he died someday. But he decided to give it to Jesus instead.

Jesus' body was placed inside Joseph's special tomb. A big ROCK was rolled in front of the cave, so no one could get in.

Some of the Pharisees and Sadducees went to Pilate and said, "What if Jesus' friends move the rock and take His body, and then say Jesus is alive again? That would cause a lot of trouble for you!"

That WOULD cause a lot of trouble, Pilate thought. So Pilate put guards outside the tomb to make sure no one moved the stone.

Jesus died on a Friday. All day Saturday His body lay in Joseph's tomb, and His friends were very, VERY sad.

Early Sunday morning, two of Jesus' friends came to visit the tomb. They were both women named **MARY**. Neither of them was Jesus' mother though. Mary was a popular name back then too.

The two Marys were very sad. They missed Jesus very much. They had brought **SPICES** and **PERFUME** to put on Jesus' body, which is something people did long ago.

"But how will we roll away the heavy stone?" they wondered.

Just as the two Marys were wondering what to do, **BOOM**! The ground shook. Then an angel appeared right in front of them. The angel rolled the stone away from the grave. He looked toward the Roman guards, who were so scared they probably fainted and fell on the ground!

Then the angel looked at the two Marys and SMILED.

"Don't be afraid," he said. "I know you are looking for Jesus. But He isn't here. Jesus isn't dead anymore. He is alive!"

The two Marys couldn't believe what they were hearing! *Jesus was alive?*

As they turned to go tell everyone what had happened, the two Marys bumped right into someone.

It was JESUS! Seeing Jesus filled their hearts with joy!

"Don't be afraid," Jesus said. "Go tell My disciples that I am alive again! Tell them they will see Me too!"

And that is exactly what happened. Jesus appeared to **ALL** His disciples. He explained to them why He'd had to die. He told them the great news that death had no power in God's kingdom.

Then Jesus told His friends it was time for Him to leave. From now on, spreading the kingdom of God would be **THEIR** job.

"But we need Your help!" His friends said.

Jesus smiled. "You will have My help. I will send you a Helper, who will fill you with **POWER**. The power of God! And you will do the kinds of amazing things you've seen Me do!"

And then Jesus rose up into the sky and disappeared!

The disciples were amazed. **AND** a little confused. *How would they spread the kingdom of God without Jesus? Who was this "Helper" Jesus was going to send? And how would he help?*

Jesus' friends didn't have answers to any of these questions, but they were about to get them in a big, big way.

HE IS ALIVE!
FAMILY CONNECTION

MATTHEW 28

EVERYDAY TRUTH

Jesus' kingdom power is alive in me!

TALK

How do you think Jesus' friends felt when they saw Him again after His death?

What does it mean to believe in Jesus' kingdom power?

Dear God . . .

PRAY

Dear God, thank You that Jesus is alive and an active part of our lives today! May we choose every day to believe in Your kingdom power! Amen.

ACTS, LETTERS, AND REVELATION

The rest of the New Testament makes up the next chapter in the story of God's rescue plan to save the world.

ACTS, LETTERS, and REVELATION follow Jesus' disciples on the mission He gave them before He left the earth. Jesus told His disciples it was now THEIR mission to preach and teach the good news and make more disciples. And that is still our mission today.

When Jesus went back up to heaven, He left a Helper— His Spirit. His Spirit is STILL what gives us power today. Because the Spirit lives in us, just like the disciples, we are God's messengers to the world. Our relationship with God, once broken, has been FIXED, so now we can share the LIGHT and love of Jesus.

We join with the disciples in the greatest mission of all time— to tell EVERYONE we meet, EVERYWHERE we go, about God's great love.

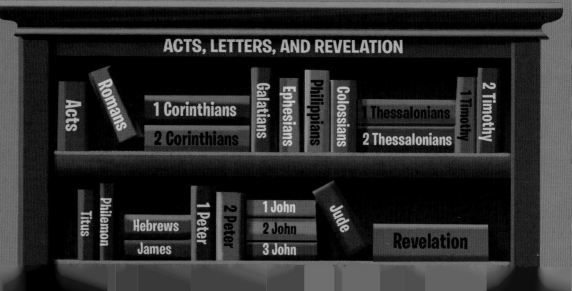

ACTS, LETTERS, AND REVELATION

Acts
Romans
1 Corinthians
2 Corinthians
Galatians
Ephesians
Philippians
Colossians
1 Thessalonians
2 Thessalonians
1 Timothy
2 Timothy

Titus
Philemon
Hebrews
James
1 Peter
2 Peter
1 John
2 John
3 John
Jude
Revelation

The Gospels showed us that JESUS is God's rescue plan to fix His broken relationship with people. In the rest of the New Testament, the disciples preach that GOOD NEWS and teach us how to live in this fixed relationship with God. The key to all of it is the Holy Spirit in us. Here's what the rest of the New Testament tells us:

The Holy Spirit gives us the power to preach the good news and make new disciples (Acts 1:8).

God's Holy Spirit changes us from the inside out, just like He changed Paul (Galatians 5:16–26).

One day, heaven and earth will come together in full bloom. We will live with God—the Father, Son, and Holy Spirit—and they will forever be our light (Revelation 21:22–24).

GOD'S SUPER HELPER

For Jesus' friends, there was good news and bad news.

The good news: Jesus was alive!

The bad news: Jesus was leaving.

Now it was up to **THEM** to spread the word about God's kingdom. As soon as Jesus told them this, He disappeared into the sky.

But there was still more news—good news **AND** bad news.

More good news: He promised to send them a helper!

More bad news: They had no idea who that helper was, or how he would help them.

And worse, Jesus' friends were **SCARED**. The Jewish leaders—the Sadducees and Pharisees—had arrested Jesus. *What if they decided to arrest Jesus' friends too?*

All of Jesus' friends were meeting together to pray. They were trying not to attract too much attention, so they wouldn't get in trouble.

One day passed. Then two days. Then three.

There was no sign of the "helper" that Jesus had promised them.

Four days passed. Five days. Six days. Nothing.

And then . . .

BOOM!
It was the tenth day since Jesus had left, and all his friends were praying together in one big room. Suddenly, a sound like a huge wind filled the house! It was pretty weird. But then things got even **WEIRDER**.

Little flames of fire—not actual fire, but something that looked like fire—appeared in the air and came down over each one of their heads while they prayed!

It was the **HOLY SPIRIT**! The Spirit of God! *Remember when Jesus was baptized?* Something that looked like a dove came down from the sky and rested on Jesus. It was the Spirit of God, coming to show that God's power was with Jesus.

And now the same thing was happening to Jesus' friends. These little flames of fire were a sign that God's power was now with each one of them!

What kind of power?

Well, the first thing that happened was that everyone in the room began speaking in different languages—languages they didn't even know! This was really helpful, because Jews who spoke many different languages were visiting Jerusalem that week from all over the Roman world. Suddenly all these visitors heard Jesus' friends speaking to them in their own language!

Then the Holy Spirit gave Jesus' disciple Peter the **POWER** to stand up and speak an amazing message about who Jesus was. After Peter proclaimed the good news that day, nearly 3,000 people who heard him speak became followers of Jesus!

Suddenly Jesus' disciples, the same ones who had been hiding together to stay out of trouble, were **BRAVELY** talking about Jesus all over Jerusalem.

Stop talking about Jesus or we'll arrest you too!" the Sadducees and Pharisees threatened. But the disciples didn't care. Filled with God's power, they were now the **BRAVEST** people on earth!

This wasn't the first time God's Spirit had filled someone with power. Kings like Saul and David had been filled with the Spirit of God. And some of Israel's judges and prophets were filled with God's power when there was a big job to do.

But before now, only certain people at certain times were filled with the Spirit of God. And if they disobeyed God, like King Saul did, God's Spirit was taken away.

This was very different. Jesus didn't just send the Holy Spirit to help a few special people do a few special things. This was much better than that! Now, for the first time ever, God's Spirit and God's power were available to **ALL** of Jesus' friends. And not just for a little while. **FOREVER**.

Yep, Jesus changed **EVERYTHING**. He didn't leave His friends alone. Instead, He gave them a "superpower"—the power of the Holy Spirit—so they could go out and change the world.

GOD'S SUPER HELPER
FAMILY CONNECTION

ACTS 2

TRICKY BITS

Who is our Helper?

Remember the Trinity? God the Father, God the Son, and God the Holy Spirit. The Holy Spirit is our Helper. When we give our hearts to Jesus, He puts His Holy Spirit inside us. When we need help, we can stop to listen or feel what He is saying or how He is leading us.

TALK

Why do you think God used fire to show His super power?

How can you use God's super power in your life?

> **Dear God . . .**

PRAY

Dear God, thank you for sending us a super Helper and filling us with Your super power so we can spread the good news of your love and rescue plan! Amen.

297

BIG CHANGES
FOR SAUL

Now it was time to spread the good news about Jesus all over the Roman world. *But who should do it? Who was the right person for such a big job?*

Peter?

Everyone looked to Peter as the leader of Jesus' followers. Filled with God's power, Peter was **BRAVE** and **SMART**. But Peter wasn't a Roman citizen. That meant it would be hard for him to travel throughout the Roman world. Besides, Peter had only lived in Israel, so he didn't know very much about the rest of the Roman world.

If Peter wasn't the right one, who was?

God had someone very special in mind for this very special job. A guy named **SAUL**.

You're probably thinking, *But Saul was the king of Israel a thousand years ago! How could he still be alive?*

This is a different Saul. Like Joseph and Mary, Saul was a popular name back then. But we don't usually call this guy "Saul." Saul was his Hebrew name, the name all his Jewish friends called him. Outside of Israel, his friends called him by his Greek name. His Greek name was . . . **PAUL**.

Heard of him? Yep, he's pretty famous. A lot of people are named Paul today, and that name became popular because of this famous guy named Paul.

Paul was a **PHARISEE**. Yes, one of the Jewish leaders who were really, really concerned about following the rules. **ALL** the rules. The Pharisees thought Jesus was breaking rules, so they worked together with the Sadducees to have Jesus arrested.

Paul was **SO** concerned about the rules that after Jesus died he made it his job to arrest as many of Jesus' friends as he could. Paul was an **ENEMY** of Jesus!

Until one day when something really crazy happened.

Paul was traveling to a town called Damascus, hoping to find more of Jesus' friends to arrest. As he was walking down the road, suddenly a **BRIGHT LIGHT** from the sky hit him right in the face, and he heard a voice speaking to him from heaven!

In Hebrew, the Jewish language, the voice said, "Saul, Saul, why are you trying to hurt Me?"

Paul was so surprised he fell down on the ground.

"Who are you?" he asked.

Then the voice said, "I am Jesus—the one you are trying to hurt."

JESUS was talking to Paul!

When Paul stood up, he couldn't see **ANYTHING**. He was totally blind! Jesus told him to go on with his friends to Damascus anyway and wait there.

In Damascus there lived a man named Ananias, who was a follower of Jesus. One day Jesus showed up in a dream and told Ananias to go find Paul.

Ananias was **CONFUSED**. He had heard of Paul, and he knew Paul wanted to arrest all of Jesus' friends!

"Why would you want me to find him?" Ananias asked. "He's mean!"

But Jesus said, "This is the one I'm going to use to spread the good news about Me to everyone! To Jews and Gentiles—and even to kings!"

So Ananias trusted Jesus and went to find Paul.

As soon as Ananias found Paul, he touched him—and immediately Paul could see again! And right then, Paul became a **FOLLOWER** of Jesus and started running around Damascus, yelling, "Jesus is the Son of God!"

Just like that, Paul went from being Jesus' **ENEMY** to becoming Jesus' **FRIEND**. And now Paul was ready to turn the Roman world upside down!

BIG CHANGES FOR SAUL
FAMILY CONNECTION

ACTS 9

EVERYDAY TRUTH

God will open my eyes to see His truth so I can tell the world.

TALK

Why do you think God blinded Paul and then healed him?

What are some ways God can prepare us to be His messengers?

Dear God . . .

PRAY

Dear God, thank You for always working to help us become better messengers of Your good news. Amen.

A VISION FOR EVERYONE

Filled with God's power, the disciples

talked about Jesus everywhere they went. And they performed miracles, just like Jesus did. Peter and the others **HEALED** people when they prayed in the name of Jesus.

A couple of times, when the Sadducees locked them up in prison, an angel came to bust them out. Then they went right back to talking about Jesus again. Jews all over Jerusalem were hearing about Jesus, and many of them were deciding **THEY** wanted to be friends with Jesus too!

More and more Jews in Jerusalem were following Jesus. *But what about the people who weren't Jews? All the other people of the world—people the Jews called "Gentiles"—could* **THEY** *be friends with Jesus? Could they be the children of God too?*

Ever since the days of Abraham, Isaac, and Jacob, the Jewish people had enjoyed a **SPECIAL** relationship with God. But God had promised Abraham something. From Abraham's family—from Israel—would come a blessing for the **WHOLE** world. *Remember that promise?*

Not a blessing only for Israel. A blessing "for the whole world."

None of Jesus' disciples had given this much thought. God's love wasn't for **EVERYONE**. It was just for the children of Israel. *Right?*

Then Peter had a dream.

Well, it wasn't really a dream—it was a **VISION**. *What's a vision?* It's like a dream, only you aren't sleeping when you have it.

One day Peter was on his roof, praying. *Have you ever prayed on your roof before? No?* That's probably because you don't live when Peter lived. Back in Peter's day, roofs were flat. People used their roofs the same way we use back porches and patios today.

Peter was praying on his roof when **SUDDENLY** he had a vision. In this vision, God showed him something that looked like a giant sheet being lowered from the sky.

Inside the giant sheet were all the animals the Israelites weren't supposed to eat, according to the laws God gave to Moses, like **PIGS** and **CAMELS** and **RABBITS**.

Then a voice said, "Get up, Peter! Kill one of these animals and eat!"

Peter, who had always followed the Jewish rules about food, said, "No! I have never eaten anything unclean!"

But then the voice said, "Don't call anything unclean that God has made clean."

Peter was very confused. *Don't call anything unclean that God has made clean? What did* **THAT** *mean?* Peter had no idea.

Just then, three men knocked on Peter's door. They were the servants of a Roman army commander named CORNELIUS.

Cornelius wasn't Jewish. He was a Gentile. Still, Cornelius loved God, and God had given Cornelius a dream of his own. In his dream an angel had told him to send men to get Peter. The angel even told Cornelius where Peter would be staying.

Now Peter knew what his vision meant. Up to that time, Peter and the other disciples had NEVER talked to Gentiles, because they believed they were "unclean." Like the animals the Israelites weren't supposed to eat.

But God was telling Peter not to treat anyone like that. Both Jews AND Gentiles were God's children!

So Peter went to see Cornelius and his family. He told them all about **JESUS** and the good news. And Cornelius's whole family became followers of Jesus that day! Then Cornelius and his family were filled with God's power. They began speaking in different languages, just like the Jewish believers.

Peter and the other disciples were **AMAZED**. For the first time they realized that the good news about Jesus was for **EVERYONE**! Jesus was the blessing God had promised Abraham—the blessing for the **WHOLE WORLD**!

A VISION FOR EVERYONE
FAMILY CONNECTION

ACTS 10

EVERYDAY TRUTH

God loves us all the same!

TALK

What was God trying to tell Peter in his vision?

Why do you think it's important to treat all God's children the same?

Dear God . . .

PRAY

Dear God, thank You for loving all of Your children the same! Please help us to love all people with Your unconditional love. Amen.

PAUL'S TRAVELS

God chose Paul to spread the good news about Jesus all over the Roman world.

Why Paul?

First of all, Paul was really, really **SMART**. Remember, he was a Pharisee, and Pharisees were smart because they spent years studying and memorizing God's laws and the stories of Israel. But Paul was even smarter than the average Pharisee. Paul was like a super-Pharisee!

Paul spoke Hebrew, the language of Israel, so Paul could talk to **EVERYONE** in Israel about God and His Son, Jesus. But Paul also spoke Greek, the language of the Roman Empire, because he had grown up in Tarsus, which was part of the Roman world.

There was one more thing that made Paul **PERFECT** for this job. He was a Roman citizen.

Today, if you're born in a country, you are automatically a **CITIZEN** of that country. You get the special rights and freedoms of being a citizen of that country.

But in Paul's day, it was very special to be a **ROMAN** citizen. Very few people in the Roman Empire, and almost no Jews, were actually citizens. Being a citizen was a huge help to Paul as he began sharing the good news. *How?*

Well, if you were a Roman citizen, you could travel **ANYWHERE** in the Roman Empire without any trouble at all. So Paul could go anywhere and talk to **ANYONE** about Jesus.

If Paul was ever arrested for talking about Jesus, he couldn't be killed the way Jesus was killed, because he was a Roman citizen.

And finally, if a Roman citizen was arrested and put on trial and didn't think the trial was fair, he could "appeal to Caesar." The trial would end, and he would be taken to Rome to appear before Caesar himself, the king of the whole Roman Empire!

There was no bigger king than Caesar, and all Paul had to do to go see him was say, "I appeal to Caesar!" Which, a few years later, is exactly what he did.

Paul started traveling all over the Roman world telling people about Jesus. Jesus followers started popping up everywhere. They began meeting together in groups that we now call **CHURCHES**.

Soon, there was a new name for these followers of Jesus. Since they wanted to be just like Jesus Christ, people started calling them **CHRISTIANS**, which means "little Christs."

Paul **LOVED** telling people about Jesus, even though it didn't always go very well. Two times Paul was on a ship that sank in the sea.

He was attacked by groups of people who wanted him to stop talking about Jesus. He was bitten by a poisonous snake. He was arrested and thrown in jail.

But even in the hard times, Paul was filled with **JOY**. God gave Paul the strength to be happy if he was full, or if he was hungry. If he had money, or if he had none. If he was free, or if he was in prison. No matter what happened, God was with Paul. God was Paul's **FRIEND**. And Paul was happy.

The Pharisees and Sadducees, on the other hand, were **NOT** happy. Paul was supposed to be arresting Jesus' followers, and instead more and more of them were showing up all over the Roman Empire!

The Pharisees and Sadducees got the Roman governor to arrest Paul because he was a troublemaker. While Paul was in jail, he discovered the Pharisees were planning to kill him. So Paul decided to do something really bold.

"**I APPEAL TO CAESAR**!" he said.

And sure enough, because he was a Roman citizen, Paul was put on a boat and sent all the way to Rome, the capital of the Roman Empire. Now all Paul had to do was wait for his turn, and he would get to tell Caesar all about Jesus!

Caesar, though, was a little busy.

Paul sat in a Roman jail, waiting to talk to Caesar, for at least two whole years.

What did he do while he waited? What would you do?

While he was waiting to meet with Caesar, Paul wrote letters. **LOTS** of letters. Some of which you've probably read!

PAUL'S TRAVELS
FAMILY CONNECTION

ACTS 25

FUN FACTS

Paul took four important missionary journeys during his life as a messenger of God's good news. He visited more than forty-five cities throughout his ministry of over thirty years. For a map of Paul's travels, turn to page 316.

TALK

What are some reasons God chose Paul to spread His good news?

Why do you think Paul was able to have joy, no matter what?

Dear God . . .

PRAY

Dear God, thank You that we can have joy in good times and bad. Show us ways we can joyfully share Your good news with others. Amen.

PAUL'S MISSIONARY JOURNEYS

JOURNEYS	DATE	TRAVEL PARTNER	WRITINGS
—— First Journey	AD 48–49	Barnabas	Possibly Galatians
—— Second Journey	AD 51–53	Silas	1 & 2 Thessalonians
—— Third Journey	AD 54–57	Various Disciples	1 & 2 Corinthians, Galatians, Romans
—— Journey to Rome	AD 59–60	Julius the Centurion and other prisoners	Ephesians, Philippians, Colossians, Philemon

"**Therefore go and make disciples of all nations . . .**"
Matthew 28:19 (NIV)

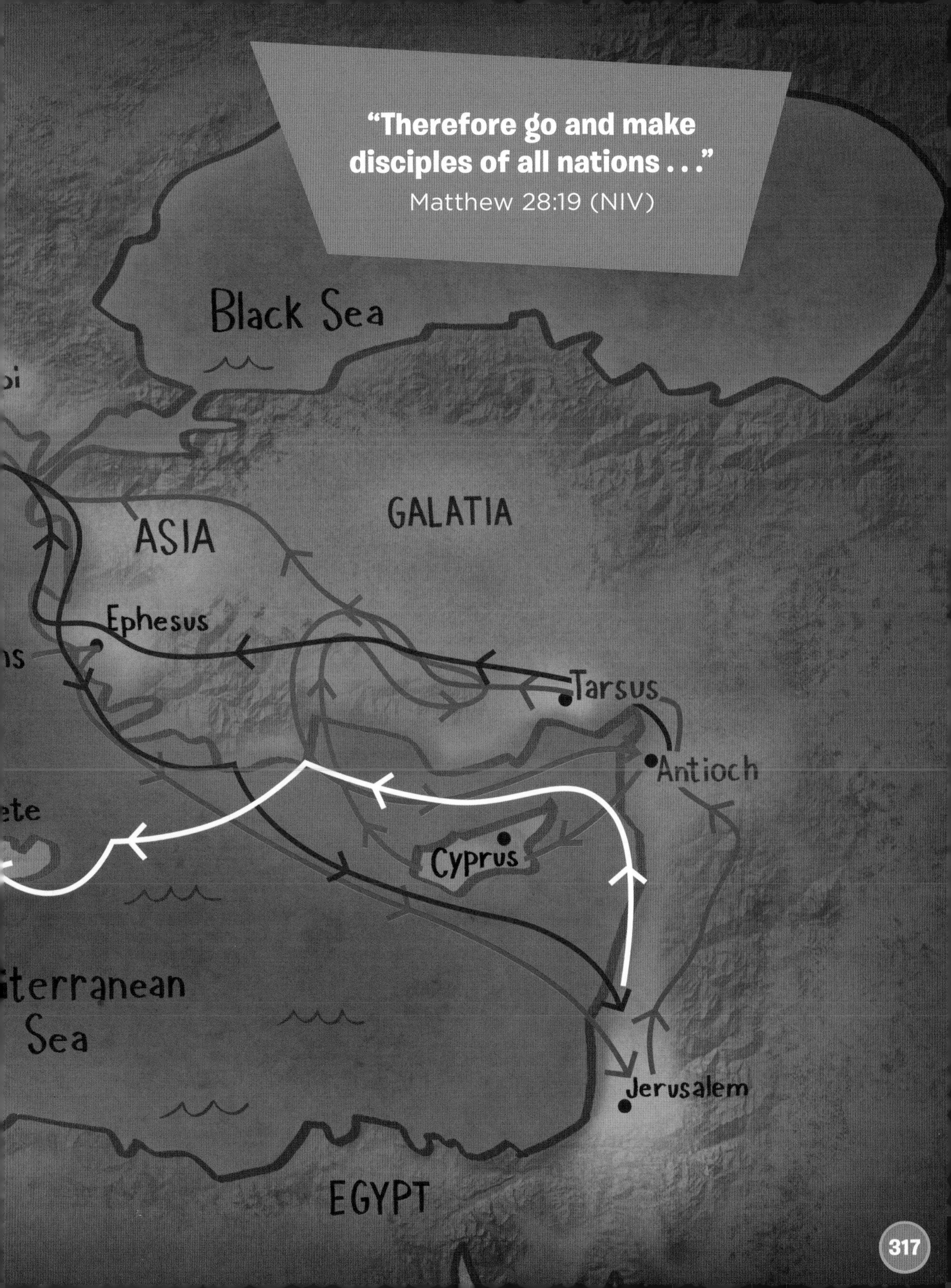

Black Sea

GALATIA

ASIA

Ephesus

Tarsus

Antioch

Cyprus

rete

iterranean
Sea

Jerusalem

EGYPT

PAUL'S LETTERS

Paul wrote letters while he was in prison.

He also wrote letters when he wasn't in prison. Paul wrote **LOTS** of letters. We don't know exactly how many he wrote, but thirteen of his letters are in the Bible, and we can read them whenever we want. Let's take a look at them.

ROMANS is Paul's longest letter. It was written to the Christians in Rome to explain how the world is broken and how Jesus came to fix it. If you want to learn what Christians believe, the book of Romans is a great place to start.

FIRST AND SECOND CORINTHIANS are two letters written to the Christians in the city of Corinth. Corinth was a big city with mean people, and some of the meanness was creeping into the church. So in his letters, Paul reminded the Corinthians how Christians should live. "Live like this, not like that. Don't be mean!" Paul explained what **REAL** Christian love looks like—not the mushy, gushy kind you see on TV. Christian love is patient and kind and puts other people first.

GALATIANS and **EPHESIANS** are letters written to the churches in Galatia and Ephesus. Galatians explains how Christians are free from the Jewish law. *Remember all the laws about what to eat and how to dress? The laws practiced so carefully by the Pharisees?* Paul wrote in Galatians that Jesus **FREED** us from those laws. Instead, Jesus asks us to love God and love others. Having a heart that loves God and loves others is much more important than what we eat and what we wear!

Ephesians talks all about **RECONCILIATION**. *Reconciliation* is a fancy word that means "to fix a broken relationship." *Remember Adam and Eve?* Their relationship with God was **BROKEN** by sin. Our relationship with God is broken by sin too. That's what Jesus came to fix, Paul says. Jesus came to reconcile the **WHOLE WORLD** to God, and to help us reconcile with each other. Fixing broken relationships is really important to God!

PHILIPPIANS is a letter all about joy. When he thought about God's love, Paul was so happy he couldn't stop smiling. Even though he was in prison! God showed Paul how to be happy no matter what was going on in his life. *Wouldn't you like to have joy like Paul?* Reading Philippians is a good place to start!

COLOSSIANS is a letter Paul wrote to fix some bad teaching that was popping up in the church in a city called Colossae. Sometimes people got confused about how to follow Jesus or about who God is and what He wants from us, so Paul wrote letters to remind them.

FIRST AND SECOND THESSALONIANS are letters written to the Christians in Thessalonica. Some of the Christians there were confused about Jesus coming back. *When would He return? What would it be like?* Paul wrote to encourage them that Jesus **WOULD** come back someday to make everything right and good, even though we don't know when.

FIRST AND SECOND TIMOTHY and **TITUS** are letters written to two young men, Timothy and Titus, who were learning how to lead churches and be pastors. Paul wrote to give them lots of advice. He told Timothy to always trust in God and to run away from evil. He told Titus to be honest, so he would set a good example for others.

And finally, **PHILEMON** is a tiny little letter written to a man named—*you guessed it*—Philemon. Philemon had a servant named Onesimus, who ran away from Philemon and took some things that didn't belong to him. Onesimus had met Paul and had become a follower of Jesus. Paul helped Philemon and Onesimus reconcile, or fix, their broken relationship. He asked Philemon to forgive Onesimus and take him back, not as a servant, but as a brother in Jesus!

No matter what you're going through in your life, Paul's letters can help you. From how to live worthy of Jesus to how to stand up for Jesus even when it's **HARD**, there's encouragement and instruction in these thirteen letters for everyone!

PAUL'S LETTERS
FAMILY CONNECTION

ROMANS-PHILEMON

FUN FACTS

Epistle is a fancy word for "letter." It comes from the Greek word *epistole*, which means—*you guessed it*—"letter." Of the thirteen epistles we've learned about, nine were written by Paul to encourage the churches he visited in different cities.

TALK

What does Colossians say real Christian love looks like?

What does Ephesians say about our broken relationship with God?

Dear God . . .

PRAY

Dear God, thank You for showing us how to be a follower of Jesus through Paul's letters. Help us to live out the truth we find in the Bible. Amen.

FROM WRONG TO RIGHT

We are justified by grace through faith!" According to Paul, this is really important to know. So important that he says it over and over.

"We are justified by grace through faith!"

Great. *But what does it mean? What is "justified"? What is "grace"? And what is "faith"?* Let's dive in and see if we can figure out why Paul says this is so important!

To **JUSTIFY** someone is to say that what the person has done is good and right. No need for punishment—what the person has done is the right thing to do!

Imagine if someone wants to put you in jail because you walked out of a store with a bunch of bananas. "You **STOLE** those bananas!" they yell. "Put her in jail!" They put a sticker on you that says, "**WRONG**!"

But then the owner of the store runs out and says, "No, she paid for the bananas! It is **RIGHT** for her to take them home!" The storeowner takes off the "**WRONG**" label and puts on another sticker that says, "**RIGHT**."

Now you have been **JUSTIFIED**. You are not a banana thief. The storeowner said that what you did was right.

Get it?

Grace is a word that means "undeserved favor." Favor means kindness. So, grace, or "undeserved favor," means you have been given a kindness—a gift—that you didn't earn.

If your neighbor gives you ten dollars after you mow her yard, have you earned that money?

Yes. You mowed the yard. You earned the money.

But what if you don't mow the yard, and your neighbor gives you ten dollars anyway, just because she likes you? Now did you earn the money?

Nope. You didn't **EARN** the money. The ten dollars was a **GIFT** you didn't earn.

And that's what **GRACE** is. A gift you didn't earn.

What is the gift Paul talked about that we haven't earned? Well, it's much better than ten dollars. The gift we haven't earned is **FRIENDSHIP** with God. It's the forever-kind-of-life with Jesus, in a world without sadness and sickness—a world made **RIGHT**!

Remember, sin keeps us **AWAY** from God. When we ignore God and do whatever we want to do—like when we put ourselves first instead of putting other people first—we break our friendship with God. We can't have the forever-kind-of-life with Jesus.

To be friends with God again, we need to have our labels changed from "wrong" to "right." From "enemy of God" to "friend of God."

But we can't change our own labels. That's why Jesus came. That's why He died on the cross. **JESUS** took our labels that said **WRONG**, and put them on Himself, even though He hadn't done anything wrong. Then He took His own label that said **RIGHT**, and put it on us. Jesus justified us!

We are justified by grace through faith."

What's faith? It's simple. **FAITH** is trusting that Jesus can do what He says He can do. Faith is **BELIEVING** the good news about Jesus and the forever-kind-of-life we can have with Him.

Our labels are changed from "wrong" to "right," even though we didn't earn it, because we have faith in Jesus and trust Him with our lives.

To Paul, **NOTHING** was more important than this!

FROM WRONG TO RIGHT
FAMILY CONNECTION

EPHESIANS 2:1-10

EVERYDAY TRUTH

Because I have faith in God, He changes me from the inside out!

TALK

What does *grace* mean?

How does our relationship with God change our "label"?

Dear God . . .

PRAY

Dear God, Your grace and love are so much more than we deserve. Thank you for inviting us into a forever-kind-of-life with Jesus. Amen.

THE FRUIT OF THE SPIRIT

Have you ever seen an apple tree? *What kind of fruit comes from an apple tree?*

That's right. Apples!

Paul talked about fruit in his letters. But he didn't mean apples and oranges. That wasn't the kind of fruit he was talking about.

Paul talked about the fruit of **SIN**. *What grows out of sin?* Bad things. Selfishness. Anger. Greed. All the bad things in the world are the fruit of sin. Yuck.

But then Paul talked about the fruit that comes from the Spirit of God. When we follow Jesus and we're filled with God's Spirit, the fruit that grows out of us changes!

Instead of anger, we show **LOVE**. Instead of selfishness, we help others. Instead of being greedy, we **SHARE**.

Paul said, "The fruit of the Spirit is love, joy, peace, patience, kindness, goodness, faithfulness, gentleness, and self-control."

Wow. That's some good fruit!

FAITHFULNESS

SELF-CONTROL   PEACE

LOVE   GOODNESS

PATIENCE   JOY

KINDNESS   GENTLENESS

331

There was one person who showed all of this fruit perfectly. He was perfectly loving, perfectly kind, perfectly good . . . the whole list!

Do you know who it was?

It was **JESUS**.

That's why people loved to be around Him!

And here's the really good news. If we follow Jesus, the Spirit of God will turn us into people who are like Jesus too. We can be filled with love and joy and peace! *Why was Paul filled with joy even while he was in prison?* Because the Spirit of God was **CHANGING** Paul to be like Jesus!

Isn't that awesome?

When Jesus was on Earth, He told His friends that if they loved Him, they would **FOLLOW** His commands. They would live like He lived. You might think He was saying, "You **HAVE** to do what I do."

But that's not it at all.

What Jesus was really saying was this: "If you love Me, you'll **WANT** to do what I do. What you want will **CHANGE**, by the **POWER** of the Holy Spirit!"

This is really great news. Sin can whisper in our ears, telling us to do more and more bad things. Jesus breaks the **POWER** of sin. Sin can't boss us around anymore!

How does this work? If we make a decision to follow Jesus, do we wake up the next day and start acting just like Jesus?

Not exactly. Becoming like Jesus takes time. In fact, it will take your **WHOLE** life! We become more and more like Jesus, little by little, every day.

How?

By practicing. There are some things we do together with other Christians, and some things we do on our own every day.

Together, we're part of the **CHURCH**. We meet together, sing together, praise God together, and work to help others together.

On our own, we read the Bible. We **PRAY**. We set aside time to think about God, talk to God, and listen to Him.

When we ask God to help us, and then practice **EVERY DAY**, we become more and more like Jesus. More loving. More joyful. More patient. The forever-kind-of-life shows up in us!

Following Jesus doesn't mean we focus on God's rules. It means we focus on **GOD**. And when we focus on God—when we walk with Jesus—the Holy Spirit changes our hearts.

We become more like Jesus and grow good fruit every day!

THE **FRUIT** OF THE **SPIRIT**
FAMILY CONNECTION

GALATIANS 5:22-23

EVERYDAY TRUTH

When I follow Jesus,
my life is full of
good fruit!

TALK

What nine traits are the fruits of the Spirit?

Which trait would you like to grow more of in your life?

Dear
God . . .

PRAY

Dear God, thank You for filling us with Your Spirit so we can grow good fruit in our lives. Amen.

HOW DOES
IT END?

"How does it end?"

Isn't that what you wonder when you're reading or listening to a good story?

"How does it end?"

All of Jesus' friends knew they were in a good story—an **AMAZING** story. The story of God's great rescue plan! A plan to put everything right. Destroy sin. End evil. Reconcile the whole world to God.

Remember the word reconcile? It means "to fix a broken relationship." And that's exactly what God wants to do for all of us.

Ever since Adam and Eve first sinned, when they decided to trust that sneaky snake in the garden instead of trusting God, our relationships have been **BROKEN**.

First through Abraham, then the nation of Israel, then Jesus and the church, God has been working throughout history to save us from our brokenness.

"How does it end?"

That's the question the apostle **JOHN** was asking before he wrote the book of **REVELATION**.

John was one of Jesus' closest friends, and after Jesus left, John had traveled and preached so much that he was finally arrested and sent to a small island to live alone where he couldn't bother anyone with all this "Jesus" talk.

While John was on that island, he kept **ASKING** the question, "How does it end?"

And God showed him.

Remember Peter and his vision of a sheet coming down from the sky, filled with animals? Now it was John's turn to have a vision or two. Or three. Or four. A whole bunch of visions, giving clues to the end of God's story!

Like Peter's vision, some of those clues were pretty weird.

There were lamps on stands and lions and lambs, and strange creatures with wings, and a **DRAGON**!

John saw stars fall from the sky. And hailstones and earthquakes! Then things got even crazier.

John had visions of monsters from the sea and giant locusts with long hair and lion teeth!

Just like Peter's vision of the sheet and the animals, John's visions were filled with **SYMBOLS**. *What was going on? What was John supposed to think of all this?*

God was giving John **PICTURES** that told a **STORY** of when God would set everything right. When God would end all the evil ways people hurt each other. When God's enemies would be defeated once and for all!

Some of John's visions were pretty freaky. *But what do they mean?*

God is going to destroy evil and set things right. He's been **WAITING**—waiting for us to have a chance to become His friends. But He will only wait so long. There will be signs and warnings, and then God will step in and end all evil.

In those final days, that sneaky snake, Satan, will try to hurt God's friends. But that snake has already lost. He's been beaten by the Lamb of God. By Jesus!

And in the very end, we will see a new heaven and a new earth. Everything will be **RESTORED**. Reconciled. Cleaned of all evil. At last, the kingdom of God in full **BLOOM**!

And heaven and earth will be together! In his visions, John saw a new city where we will live with God. In the center of the city is the tree of life from the Garden of Eden, bringing **HEALING** to all God's friends.

The story that started with a garden ends with a **GARDEN CITY**. The city of God. Where there is no sickness, no tears, no bullies, and no death. A new Earth, cleaned of sin and evil, where we will live, work, eat, play, sing, and dance with the God who made us and who loves us very much!

Don't you want to come?

HOW DOES IT END?
FAMILY CONNECTION

REVELATION

TRICKY BITS

What will heaven be like?

The Bible provides many clues about what the new heaven and the new earth will be like. But the truth is, no one really knows for sure. We can trust that it will be wonderful—free of sadness (Revelation 21:4) and full of joy (Psalm 16:11)—the way God always intended His creation to be.

TALK

What story was God telling John through his visions?

What does Revelation tell us will happen to heaven and earth at the end of God's story?

Dear God . . .

PRAY

Dear God, thank You that we can look forward to living together with You someday. When life is hard and we need hope, help us remember how the story ends. Amen.